She Speaks / He Listens

She Speaks / He Listens

Women on the French Analyst's Couch

Elaine Hoffman Baruch
Lucienne Juliette Serrano

Routledge
New York and London

Published in 1996 by
Routledge
29 West 35th Street
New York, NY 10001

Published in Great Britain by
Routledge
11 New Fetter Lane
London EC4P 4EE

Copyright © 1996 by Routledge

Book Design: Jeff Hoffman

Printed in the United States of America on acid-free paper.

Library of Congress Cataloging-in-Publication Data

Baruch, Elaine Hoffman.
     She speaks / he listens: women on the French analyst's couch /
    Elaine Hoffman Baruch, Lucienne Juliette Serrano.
      p. cm.
    Includes bibliographical references and index.
    ISBN 0-415-91126-5 (hb). — ISBN 0-415-91127-3 (pb)
    1. Psychoanalysis and feminism—France. 2. Sex differences
    (Psychology)—France. 3. Femininity (Psychology) 4. Freud, Sigmund,
    1865-1939. 5. Lacan, Jacques, 1901- . 6. Psychoanalysts—France—
    Interviews.
    I Serrano, Lucienne J. II. Title.
    BF175.4.F45B37 1995
    155.3'33—dc20   95-44308
                                                   CIP

contents

Preface

"Turn to the poets" if you want to know more about women, wrote Freud at the end of his 1933 lecture on femininity. But coming from literature, it was to psychoanalysis that we turned for new insights on poetry. Given the gender revolution of our time, questions of sexual difference began to take on great importance for us—in literature as well as in psychoanalysis.

The importance of the European scene, especially the French one, led us on many journeys from the United States to England and France in search of analysts—and writers—who were exploring new ways of looking at women in culture. We started by questioning women analysts. This resulted not only in our book *Women Analyze Women* but also in one of us becoming an analyst herself (L.J.S.).

We did not end our search with women, however, for we rightly felt that men would have a great deal to say about the subject. After all, they always had. We have found that some male psychoanalysts themselves cling to fantasies that reveal men's psychic needs: fantasies that have played a major role in encoding women into androcentric culture. Other analysts are less self-referential and more empathetic; along with women, they are transvaluating myth, religion, philosophy, literature—and psychoanalysis itself.

What has been hidden in the subterranean depths of the unconscious, that problematic "dark continent," which belongs to all of us—men as well as women—is the power of women. While some—women as well as men—fear and deny that power, many male analysts today acknowledge their envy of women—envy of their sexuality, their maternity, and their way of being and connecting, which like the writing of great poets reconciles opposites.

Why do we turn mainly to French analysts rather than American ones to illuminate literature and questions of sexual difference? Because French psychoanalysts are steeped in mythology, philosophy, poetry. In contrast, American analysts are primarily clinical, empirical, scientific. There are, of course, exceptions. For example, Otto Kernberg brings to the American scene the richness of his origins in Vienna, his youth in South America, and, most importantly for this book, his experience and knowledge of French psychoanalysis and culture.

We wish to thank all the French analysts who participated in these interviews for giving generously of their time and of themselves. We particularly commend their courage in expressing ideas about women that might put them at risk in certain milieus. To Otto Kernberg, in this country, goes our gratitude for sharing with us his sources and ideas about French psychoanalytic theory and influence here and abroad.

We thank our editors at Routledge: Maureen MacGrogan for her warm encouragement, Alison Shonkwiler for her caring support, and Jeff Hoffman for his helpful attention. The New York Psychoanalytic Library provided an enclave of calm; there we had the welcome aid of Matthew von Unwerth. Elsewhere Elizabeth Gold always had a ready ear and a cogent response.

It is with gratitude that we acknowledge the funding of the PSC-CUNY Research Foundation for this project; we especially value the advice of Brenda Newman, Joyce Mullan, and Miriam Korman. We are particularly appreciative of Nancy Chow at York College for her constant availability and expert help in solving computer problems.

Our greatest debts are to the analytic, academic, and literary communities, both here and in France, to our many friends, and to the dear members of our families. We owe special thanks to Greg Baruch for his help with the title.

N.B. Unless otherwise stated, all translations from the French are ours.

Introduction

It wasn't too long ago that psychoanalysis was nothing but a long four-letter word to many women. But feminists are turning increasingly to psychoanalysis for an understanding of sexual differences. One reason is that, despite its reputation to the contrary, psychoanalytic theory has, almost from its inception, questioned whether anatomy is destiny. As Mikkel Borch-Jacobsen puts it:

> the real scandal of the Oedipus complex is not that there is infantile sexuality and that the child harbors incestuous and patricidal desires but that access to genital heterosexuality is not a foregone conclusion. The child is not born boy or girl, at least not from the psychical point of view; it becomes one or the other. (271)

Our main purpose in this book is to illustrate the range of some well-known French male psychoanalysts today with regard to women and sexual difference. Represented here are Gérard Pommier, Alain Didier-Weill, Patrick Guyomard, François Roustang, Serge Lebovici,

Horacio Amigorena, René Major, and Béla Grunberger, as well as the American analyst Otto Kernberg, who speaks of French influences on his own work. Our earliest interview was with François Roustang in 1988; others continued through 1994. There are other analysts we would have liked to include as well. But reality in one form or another interfered with our wish fulfillment. As it stands, our selection represents both the traditional and the avant-garde. The most influential figure in current French psychoanalysis, the one whose shadow falls across almost every figure here as well as those who are not, arousing every feeling from outrage to adoration and everything in between, is Jacques Lacan, who died in 1981. His power to arouse antithetical responses, even among feminists, is testimony both to his theoretical provocativeness and/or his charismatic persuasiveness. In our final interview, Otto Kernberg explains some of Lacan's extraordinary power.

After writing our book *Women Analyze Women: In France, England, and the United States*, which examines a new form of psychoanalysis that might be called "feminist psychoanalysis," one "that puts into question the androcentric views of culture and women" (11), we decided to look at the current trends in psychoanalytic theory and practice among influential male analysts with regard to women and chose France to begin with.

As in our other book, we use the interview format here. Given its potential for spontaneity and surprise, but also its scrutiny by the interviewee after transcription and translation, we considered this genre as the one most likely to approximate the truth. The recent lengthy trials involving Janet Malcolm and Jeffrey Masson over charges of misuse and fabrication of quotation lent support to our conviction. And yet we wondered.

In *After Bakhtin*, David Lodge writes: "The distinctive feature of the interview is what Harold Bloom would call its 'agonistic' element: the object of the interviewer is to get the interviewee to reveal or betray his authentic self, whereas the aim of interviewee is, usually, to *construct* a self that he wishes the world to see" (183). At first, we thought that this definition had little to do with our own approach and that any agonistic element in an interviewer would reveal not a general but a particular perversity, similar to Bloom's. Certainly our questions in *Women Analyze Women* had nothing of this *conscious* competitive element. Rather we wanted to catch "thought on the wing," to turn the interview into a "conversational essay" (2-3). (Maybe, come to think of it, there was some quiet competition involved in the latter concept.)

Looking back on our interviews with the male analysts, we admit that, just as analytic listening may be marked sexually, as the Paris-based Argentinian psychoanalyst Horacio Amigorena puts it, so too might analytic questioning be. Before the interviews took place we wondered how the men analysts were different from the women analysts (or were they?). We wanted to find out whether men still adhered to a phallocentric view of women and culture or whether it was possible for them to escape the "prism of gender." Would men be able to talk about women to other women without interjecting a kind of courtship dance? Would any potentially exhibitionistic analysts purposely say provocative, shocking things that they did not necessarily believe? Perhaps so, we thought, but decided that any distortions or playacting would reveal something about men in relation to women that would be important for us. In one sense, our subtext was "women analyze men," an ironic reversal of our title, for we hoped that the interviews would capture something of the flavor of the analytic session, with the male analyst as our analysand. As potential "analysts," our desire was not pure. Looking back now, the concept of *agon* begins to sound more plausible.

Interestingly enough, many of these questions began to fade once we began talking to the analysts. They no longer seemed important. On the other side, we found that we weren't the only guilty ones in any ongoing battle of the sexes. The old narratology in psychoanalysis spoke of the male Oedipal stage as if it were the only one, women's penis envy, their lack of superego, and their narcissism as justifications for androcentric culture—enough to bring about women's wrath if not their neglect of psychoanalysis. In contrast, the new male psychoanalytic narrative speaks of men's envy of women, female sexuality, women's capacity for greater connection in relationships, and their overall superiority. But some of the new psychoanalytic theory that we encountered among men could sometimes seem as misogynistic as the old. A minor but annoying leitmotif: some referred to patients using only the masculine pronoun, a rather striking use of the generic *he*, considering that we were interviewing them about women. Yet almost all claimed to be feminists, even those who saw feminism as bringing more problems to women than they had had before its latest phase. We wondered why some men seemed so willing to align themselves with feminism, when it did not seem that they were feminist at all, except perhaps in a distorted version of cultural feminism, which has recourse to traditional stereotypes of masculinity and femininity although it transvaluates them. Is there, in some men's "feminism," an echo of chivalry, of coming to the rescue of the damsel in distress? After all, it is noble and just, heroic even, to be on the side of the oppressed. What was fascinating to us was that some of the same analysts who professed themselves feminists, or at least indebted to the feminist movement, had a noticeable desire to keep the mystery of woman alive. Though we have a limited sample of analysts represented in our interviews, we can safely say that, in many of the analytic offices of Paris, the mythology of women is alive and well. However, we must add that one does not even have to cross the Seine to see this mythology put into question—by men as well as women. Some of their questions are represented here.

In the first group, images of the madonna and the whore, the femme fatale, and the eternal feminine are flourishing. As much as some men want to know about everything else, they wish to retain an aura of secrecy around women and their sexuality. Often their depiction of women sounds like something out of nineteenth-century Romanticism, with women inhabiting a place of nostalgia, a lost continent. These analysts do not believe that a new equality of the sexes can be socially constructed since they see the unconscious as a repository of infantile fantasies, a minefield of fears and longings about women that no amount of conscious reasoning can eliminate. In contrast, the other group believes that male fantasy should no longer dictate female destiny. As Julia Kristeva has written in "Women's Time": "The new generation of women is showing that its major social concern has become the socio-symbolic contract as a sacrificial contract," a "contract against their will." They are "attempting a revolt" (Moi 200). There are male analysts who are also questioning the socio-symbolic contract, and one way in which they are doing this is by deconstructing or restructuring myth. A major example is Patrick Guyomard in his reinterpretation of the place of Antigone in Lacanian theory. There are others as well.

The Analyst and the Analytic Scene

What is the *analytic scene?* A transitional space between home and the world. It is the place where the speaking subject attempts to reorganize her libidinal structure. There is no doubt that the analytic setting is a displacement that represents moving from an old place to a new one where one is at first a stranger who has to learn to speak a different language (*déparler*), one that is beyond logic, structure, constraint, that thrives on parapraxis, nonsense, gaps, silences, gestures, a language that was postmodern before postmodernism arrived. The analytic process brings/provokes emotional displacements, such as transference and countertransference, and the linguistic displacements of metaphor and metonymy, all of which allow the subject to say that she or he is, above all, a subject who desires. What we mean by desire here is what the patient's psyche longs for. The analytic scene is the only place where desire can be expressed without reservation.

In *Women Analyze Women* we spoke about the demand by the analytic patient to be born again, much like the male subject on an epic quest. But might this demand be a displacement for another faraway and unattainable moment in the analysand's life, that of her conception? Scientifically, we know that conception results from the union of two beings, but psychologically, it is the mother who looms like the sole progenitor. Why? Because what we desire to refind is that most intimate place, the body of the mother, a place of darkness and luminosity at the same time—perfect fusion, paradise, utopia.

In *Démasquer le réel* Serge Leclaire puts it differently. For him, the primal scene is displaced from the parents' bedroom to the analytic setting, which gives the analysis an incestuous essence by turning the analyst into an eroticized mother and father. We feel that the patient in her quest for the object makes of the analyst the early mother whom she couldn't see but so intensely felt. As Bice Benvenuto writes, "Transference is love for the analyst not as an object of desire, but as its cause because s/he has functioned as an *agent provocateur*, and her/his position of supposed knowledge pushes the analysand closer to a relation to a supposed 'original' love-object" (4). How will the male analyst live in this new form of parturition? Will he allow a woman patient to be the subject? Are men analysts aware of their privileged place not only within the dominant culture but also behind and above the couch—dare we say it—in the missionary position?

Contrary to a prevalent view of the analyst as a neutral sounding board, a kind of *tabula rasa* on which the patient projects her fears and desires, psychoanalytic discourse is highly emotionally marked because of the transference and countertransference. Although none of the analysts that we spoke to advocated doctor/patient sexual relationships, many saw the analyst as a potential seducer, a romantic if inaccessible lover. We wondered if the psychoanalytic office was the last outpost of romantic love, a scene of "obstacle relations," to use Adam Phillips's term. According to Lacan, "the analyst is less concerned with the supposed 'good' of the patient than with her/his Eros, as the analysand always turns into a lover in the transference, and the analytical couch turns into a place where the unhappy lover can let his/her Eros speak" (Benvenuto 6). Amigorena speaks of the seductive power of the analyst for the woman who may have never been listened to before in her life. Otto Kernberg discusses the varied responses that are possible, on both the patients' and the analysts' side, to the lures of seduction.

At his worst, the male analyst, through his envy of the mother, takes on the role of Pygmalion, fabricating his own notion of what a woman should be. In this sense he is like the "technocrat" of reproductive technology (has womb envy become womb inquiry today?) who aspires to the role of Zeus, wanting to conjure an Athena out of the test tube if not out of his own head.

The womblike enclosure of the analytic space can only be safe if the analyst respects the autonomy of the patient in all her particularities. The successful analysis offers a safe passage as well as a safe place where the patient is born from a silent transferential presence, and her own voice can express the ontological malaise of belonging to a hostile world in which being is marked by separation and difference.

Ethnopsychoanalysis and Woman as Outsider

Despite the large number of women patients and practitioners in psychoanalysis, as the other sex, women were formerly relegated to the sidelines in theory (at least after the inception of psychoanalysis). This is a situation that some analysts of different persuasions—men as well as women—are now trying to address and remedy. Furthermore, the analysis of minority patients, those outside the dominant culture, or the "over culture" as the American Indian poet Joy Harjo terms it, has recently surfaced, in an extension of the general twentieth-century movement to liberate the oppressed. Such analysis is perhaps less an issue in the United States, where medication has become the treatment of choice for those who cannot pay, and in many cases those who can, than it is elsewhere. In France, however, centers of ethnopsychiatry have sprung up around Paris, particularly in the suburb of Saint Denis, where many migrants from North Africa are settling. Among its most important practitioners are Serge Lebovici, who also treats many patients within the dominant culture, the concern of his interview with us, and Toby Nathan, who concentrates primarily on non-Occidental patients.

Influenced by Georges Devereux, who worked and wrote in the United States as well as in France, ethnopsychoanalysis stresses cultural difference and the need for its recognition in the treatment of patients. Most of the patients who come to the Centre Devereux have undergone several medical procedures without success. The ethnopsychoanalytic consultation is their last resort. The aim of ethnopsychoanalysis is to remove the patients from their pathological isolation and to bring them, through a process of mediation, to other people who share their language and culture.

Perhaps one of the most important premises of this form of psychoanalysis, which Toby Nathan writes about in the *Nouvelle revue d'ethnopsychiatrie* 24, is that "the gods have created men and not the reverse...and that different gods have created different races"; "therefore Feuerbach, Marx, and Freud were wrong" (10). According to Nathan, psychoanalysis as practiced in the West cannot be universal. In words that (perhaps) unintentionally echo the West's demonization of other cultures because they do not adhere to its beliefs, Nathan sees the analyst's so-called curing as an act of pure violence, with no therapy more violent than that which tries to cure the soul. The good doctors, he asserts, are armed to the teeth with a theory that they consider scientific: "to seize, describe, analyze—in short, to take possession of the object, always other, always fixed in its externality" *(Nouvelle revue* 22-23: 12). His words about minority groups apply even more to women—of all groups. The irony is that we do not see any special attention to women in the current ethnopsychoanalytic literature by men. Yet in some sense all women are *émigrées*, outsiders—socially, culturally, politically. Perhaps this is the price they pay for being so much the insiders, biologically and psychologically, as mothers.

In Nathan's reading of Levi-Strauss (*Nouvelle revue* 17: 14), myths of origin are biologically false but emotionally true, or as he puts it, "*logiquement justes*" (logically right). We wonder how a myth which is biologically untrue to woman's place in reproduction and the family can be rationally fair to her. Such a myth may free men from what they view as their subjection to women's bodies, but it denies mother as well as wife their place in the cultural order. Nathan is concerned with non-Occidental myths, but the same problem exists in Western ones, in which Zeus, for example, gives birth to Athena, and God creates Adam and Eve without benefit of a female consort. (Perhaps such myths counteract the psychological primacy of the mother in the child's experience and later fantasy.) If, as Nathan says, "biology and later psychoanalysis teach us to take account of the filiation of a subject [and we wonder just how much the filiation with the mother is stressed], ethnopsychiatry teaches us that what is—from the therapeutic point of view at least—the sole 'manageable' referent, is his affiliation, that is to say, the system through which he is constructed not as a hypothetical universal human, but as a cultural being" (20).

As we see it, the problem with ethnopsychoanalysis is that it makes the same mistake about women that it accuses traditional analysis of making with regard to minorities: it does not take into account women's affiliation, their unique culture. There is no question that in many respects women inhabit a different culture from men—how much because they are forced to and how much because they want to is one of the dilemmas of our time.

The term *cultural literacy* is mainly used to define an acquaintance with the major works in the Western canon. However, the phrase has recently been applied to multicultural awareness as well. In this connection, the term *literacy* may be too limited, implying a mechanical response to signs, without any probing interpretation. In addition, we find that the place of women within any given culture, Occidental or non-Occidental, is often ignored or at least neglected; this entails a type of illiteracy also. We would advocate the practice of *cultural empathy*, a quality that an analyst of intelligence and sensitivity should have, no matter what the analysand's race or sex, as Kernberg makes clear (although he does not use this term).

The Imaginary, the Symbolic, and the Real in Lacan

Most of the analysts represented here were influenced by Lacan, even those who rebelled against him. Departing from Freud, Lacan speaks about three spheres of experience: the Imaginary, the Symbolic, and the Real. Their definitions are complex and difficult. The one thing that can be said with certainty is that they differ from ordinary usage. *Imaginary* is the term that Lacan uses to describe the mirror stage ("*Le stage du miroir*"), when the child experiences a primary identification with its image in the mirror. Freud would call this "narcissistic" identification; Lacan calls it *imaginary*. The meaning is close to its etymological definition: identification with an image which is not the child itself. The Imaginary is the sphere in which the relation to individuality is indistinct because it is outside language. It is a term that is also applied to the mother/child relationship before the child is aware of separation.

Introduction to the Symbolic occurs with the Oedipal stage and is the order which allows the child to separate from the mother and to go from a fusional relationship with her—an imaginary one—to a triangular one, which includes mother and father. The child then becomes a subject distinct from both parents and enters into the world of language, sexual difference, culture, and civilization. Access to the Symbolic involves separation and castration, castration not in the usual sense, however. In the Imaginary, the child, identifying with the mother's wishes and desires, believes that he or she is the mother's phallus. In the Oedipal stage, the father deprives the child of this phallic identification when he separates mother and child. The father now represents the phallus, which is the metaphorical signifier *par excellence* for the patriarchal (phallologocentric, according to Derrida) order. However, according to Lacan, nobody possesses the phallus. It is something that we all—men as well as women—look for and never attain.

Psychoanalysis deals with the Real, which it hopes to recover but can never reach, no matter how deep the regression of the analysand. Language usually operates with structured, confined meanings (the signified), which have a close relation to the signifier (the sign that expresses this meaning). In psychoanalysis, the signified is subject to constant displacements, incessant variations. The Real is anchored at the junction of the constantly moving signified and the indistinct Imaginary.

Notes on the Analysts

Gérard Pommier

Gérard Pommier is one of the most thought provoking of the younger analysts currently on the Paris scene. "Whether they are men or women, everybody is interested in women. It is *the* subject of interest for both sexes," claims this Lacanian, who insists that "everybody loves women." Although we pointed out that historically, socially, and culturally this does not seem to be true, Pommier can be persuasive, arguing that even homosexuals "are obsessed by the question of woman and put her in the scene of their homosexuality." Pommier's explanation for women's importance in Freud's initial discovery of the unconscious and their absence from his theory of the Oedipus complex until 1930 is compelling: "The rational, the logos, is oriented toward phallic signification, which excludes feminine specificity. At the same time that there is an opening through the question and the plaint of the hysteric, there is also resistance to this knowledge." In what may come as a surprise to many, Pommier denies that Lacanian theory is phallocentric, stating that Lacan, like Freud, supported the idea of the phallus as the unique symbol for both sexes in the unconscious, a position which Pommier believes can be demonstrated with clinical examples.

When we asked Pommier if there is a symbolic system which could replace the phallic one, he responded with surprise: "Replace the phallus? Why do that?" We were equally surprised. In her treatment of Lacan's Imaginary in *Feminism and Psychoanalysis: A Critical Dictionary* (ed. Elizabeth Wright), Ellie Ragland-Sullivan suggests why for many analysts there could not be a different symbolic order:

> In Lacanian theory Woman (as a mythical cultural construct) is
> confused with mother at the level of primordial ur-objects that
> cause desire. Because these pre-specular objects—the breast,
> voice, gaze, and so on—are radically lost, but none the less con-
> stitute a foundation of the Real, the Imaginary confusion of
> mother with primordial loss rules out the possibility of Woman
> becoming a totalized Symbolic signifier, an organizing symbol of
> power. (175)

Whether women are fated to remain outsiders in the order inscribed in
Law is something now under question.

One hopeful note is Pommier's pronouncement that "Psychoanalysis has
hardly begun, especially with feminine sexuality. There is no definitive
Freudian text which allows us to consider the specificity of feminine sexual desire."

In Pommier, as well as in other Lacanians, there is a redefinition of traditional terminology that is both confusing and thought provoking. For example, on penis envy, a concept that is generally reinterpreted among these analysts, Pommier suggests a twist that involves the woman's narcissistic love.
"The erect penis is the equivalent of desire that is felt for her. She can love
the penis for that kind of desire, can love the penis the way she loves herself."
But is this envy? we might ask. Rather than wanting the penis for herself, she
wants it to be aroused by her; this is a desire for power rather than possession.

Another example of such transformation of terms involves Pommier's as
well as other Lacanians' definition of castration as both symbolic and psychological but not at all anatomical. Rather, they connect castration to separation, which in their view, is what causes desire and sexual potency. We
might question why traditional terms are retained in new readings—or mis-
readings. Then again, the history of language is filled with shifts, reversals,
transmutations of meanings. Whether they are effected this quickly or this
consciously is another matter, however. Is there a deliberate desire to mys-
tify, to keep out the uninitiated? Or is the slippage in meanings, these dar-
ing shifts and glides, a way of shattering rigid preconceptions, however
shocking these terms may have been initially?

Freud suggested that it was shame that caused women to hide their genitals and by extension, one might say, themselves, through the use of disguise and covering. But in his book *L'exception féminine*, Pommier suggests that women's use of the mask, that is, finery, adornment, concealment, makes up for a lack not in them but in men. There is something in a woman that escapes the lover's gaze. (Is that why he looks so hard?) This ungraspable something is a source of anguish, suffering, and muffled aggression for him. To hide this problematic as well as to disguise his animal origin, a source of shame as well as desire for him (since it represents the mother he both wants and fears returning to), the man turns the woman into a work of art. The mask provokes and calls up phallic *jouissance*. According to Lacanian theory, phallic *jouissance* is that sexual pleasure which belongs to both sexes. "Feminine" *jouissance*, however, refers "to that moment of sexuality which is always in excess, something over and above the phallic term which is the mark of sexual identity" (Mitchell and Rose 137).

Much has been said by psychoanalysts both in the United States and abroad about the different ways in which girls and boys resolve the Oedipus complex. (Of course, as we pointed out in *Women Analyze Women,* the term *Oedipus* in itself privileges the patriarchal.) The usual reading of these differences is that the little girl turns to the father because she has been disappointed in the mother, but she cannot have him—another source of disappointment. The little boy gives up the mother because he fears the punishment of the father, but he also identifies with him, which is a reward of sorts. In another book, *L'ordre sexuel*, Pommier notes some disturbing implications stemming from these differences for feminine and masculine desire. Feminine desire, he says, is marked by rejection and abandonment (by the father). Pommier suggests that if women feel abandoned, this provokes sadism in men, who see in feminine suffering a sign of desire that arouses their ardor. This is a far more pessimistic and sexually differentiated view than Kernberg's, for example, which holds that the two sexes arrive at the same place at the end of the journey toward love (if it is successful), however different their routes. For Pommier, "love is fundamentally bound to loss, to the impossibility of living through the body."

Alain Didier-Weill

Perhaps the most provocative statement on the place of the analyst is Alain Didier-Weill's: "I think that a prostitute with a man is in the position of the analyst." For a moment one is shocked. But then we sense a certain truth. Like the prostitute's, the psychoanalyst's couch is shared by many. And like the prostitute, he is paid for his time. But there are certain limits. One cannot ask the analyst to perform certain tricks. Actually one might, but it is doubtful that he would oblige. Still, both professionals can be seductive. And like the prostitute the analyst may be receiving his own pleasure from the session. But according to Didier-Weill, what most unites the analyst and the prostitute is that both are silent—or are supposed to be.

"I have a lot of respect for prostitutes," he adds. "I think that they know what desire is." Perhaps, but his concern was far less for their desire than for the man's. Didier-Weill's "interview" turned out to be a monologue—possibly it was an interview with himself—on the meaning of the femme fatale in men's psychology.

We are not opposed to this. We even welcomed it. Central to our examination of the analytic treatment of women is the exploration of the needs and desires of men in regard to women—including the men who treat them.

Perhaps no analyst is more concerned with men's fear of woman than is the Lacanian Didier-Weill. It is not, however, her maternal power, in Winnicott's sense, that causes the terror for him. Rather it is "the encounter with the Real" that woman represents, in contrast to man who represents the Symbolic.

Men are more terrified "when speaking in front of a woman than when in front of a gun," he claims. "A man who meets the femme fatale, this signifier in the Real, loses his control over language, babbles, as in comic films and cartoons." Because she knows—or represents—what he does not.

For Didier-Weill, language and potency are connected: "From the start, language places the woman on the side of feelings....Man is on the side of words, but words which can fail him," claims Didier-Weill. How does language place women outside words? we might ask. Like Gilbert and Gubar and unlike the Lacanians, we would assert that it is the mother who brings the child to language, who introduces her or him into the symbolic order. It seems to us that the babbling man is more on the side of feelings than the woman is. Might it be that members of the so-called rational sex can be more easily reduced to the bits and pieces of the dispersed self, are more prone to hysteria—in the layperson's sense—than women are?

It may be surprising to the American reader to find that the femme fatale, who induces this state, is still flourishing in Paris. But where else would we expect to find her? In the United States she makes only occasional guest appearances in B movies, where she now inhabits corporate offices rather than her former dwellings of the Greek isles and rocky coastlines.

For Didier-Weill, all coitus, and not just that with prostitutes, is a commercial exchange. Each sex gives the other something different. What the man receives is something of the Real from the woman. What she receives is something of the Symbolic from him. For Didier-Weill the woman makes by far the greater profit. In the sexual connection, as he sees it, the phallus (the signifier) encounters the body of the woman. Although the woman has access to the Other through the sexual relation, the man does not. In fact, he loses the symbolic Other because he merely encounters an object. This seems to be the reason why the woman enjoys the greater *jouissance*. There is only one subject in Didier-Weill's binary encounter: the man.

Didier-Weill tends to use the terms *penis* and *phallus* interchangeably, which shows how easy this slippage is, despite the claim of Lacanians (unlike the Freudians) that the phallus is not the penis, and that nobody has the phallus. In "giving" the penis, man gives a gift, says Didier-Weill. He calls this a symbolic castration. We wonder if such a fantasy stems more from fear or from male resentment?

This attitude of *ressentiment* exists only when love is not present, however. Like the troubadour poets, this analyst seems to believe that love, at least for the man, can only exist at a distance. The sexual woman "is not the muse that inspires the poet." Rather she represents one side of "the famous couple, the mother and the whore, the angel and the beast." Unlike some other male analysts, Didier-Weill sees Freud's splitting of the sexual object into one of love and one of desire as a final destination rather than as a temporary path off the route to a union of the two.

In treating Kierkegaard's *Diary of a Seducer,* Gisele Harrus-Revidi writes about the charm of virginity and the desolation (for the lover) of its loss:

> From shadow, deception (lure) and appearance, the symbolic body in its power and incomprehensible mystery is transformed in a sole instant into a castrated body. Esthetic beauty is destroyed forever because it was founded on an ethic of preservation of the sacred image of the mother. (96)

For Didier-Weill woman is either the unfindable Virgin, in which case she represents the absolute Other, or she is the whore, an object whose body is a source of pleasure but ultimate abjection. He does not see the possibility of a fusion between the two polarities as Otto Kernberg does. What causes suffering to men—and women—according to Didier-Weill, is that the man has to live between love and desire, unlike the woman, who does not have this dissociation. Americans tend to be more optimistic about love—and sex. We think that with a few minor changes, men and women can move to harmony just around the corner, to say nothing of utopia.

Patrick Guyomard

Guyomard agrees with Lacan that it is more natural for a woman to be an analyst than a man, but goes on to say, in a statement that will surely offend some: "The historic function of Lacan in psychoanalysis was to reintroduce the function of the father and therefore a certain symbolic function at a time when psychoanalysis was dominated by three awesome women: Anna Freud, Marie Bonaparte, and Lampl-de-Groot—leaving aside Melanie Klein." This sounds as if women have to be saved from women (a point that Guyomard makes in other contexts as well). But so do men. Guyomard speaks of the unconscious envy of the mother in some male analysts and the necessity for them to give up their quest for omnipotence. "Every male analyst has to mourn his relation to his own mother and to not being a mother."

Although Guyomard believes that there are times when a woman should see a woman analyst, particularly when there is a strong "investment in the maternal question," he also feels that such a woman might welcome the distance that a man represents. With a male analyst, "there is that element of resistance," a wall to lean on, as one of his patients put it.

Despite his use of the generic *he*, a practice more common in France than here, Guyomard speaks in favor of feminism. "That it causes problems to children and to men is undeniable, but these are the problems of men." In *The Gender Gap in Psychotherapy*, Joseph Pleck writes: "It is becoming increasingly recognized that one of the most fundamental questions raised by the women's movement is not a question about women at all, but rather a question about men. Why do men oppress women?"

This is a question that all the disciplines should try to answer, for it is one of the major problems of men as well as women. Guyomard's answer is perhaps more biological and social than psychoanalytical. He believes that patriarchal power was violently installed because there was always something potentially "fragile" about male identity, particularly in regard to men's tenuous role in procreation. He finds that what women won through their struggle for liberation was the right to be considered women even if they are not biological mothers. This latter source of female identity may be further undermined by advances in artificial reproduction. But there will be other sources of identity for women. In contrast, "men are going to find themselves confronted socially by a threat and a redefinition of their own identity when this question of the power of women won't be simply a fantasy but must exert itself in reality," claims Guyomard.

"One is not born a woman," said Simone de Beauvoir (267). So did Freud, for that matter, in his essay "Femininity." But as anthropologist David Gilmore points out in *Manhood in the Making*, one is not born a man either. Gilmore describes the extraordinary trials that males have to go through in almost all societies before they are judged to be men. There are already ways in which men have proved their identity without violence to women. Contrary to most feminist theory, which views women's connection to and nurturance of others as antithetical to men's self-centered behavior, Gilmore found that "manhood ideologies always include a criterion of selfless generosity, even to the point of sacrifice" (229). We might say that the symbolic order is violent to men as well as to women, although in different ways.

But in another point that some feminists will take issue with, Guyomard implicates women as accomplices in their own oppression within this symbolic system because the "destructive, dangerous, menacing" quality of so many mother/daughter and other female relationships has caused them to turn to men for their security.

It wasn't too long ago that male bonding and female divisiveness were assumed to be part of the natural order. Thanks to the most recent phase of the feminist movement, however, any such divisiveness was reassigned to the constructions of the cultural order. Now, however, there is some questioning of this transmutation. No less a feminist than Cora Kaplan, in a position similar to Guyomard's, asks "whether we may be making a dangerous over-investment in idealized fictions of maternal and sororal relations, both as a basis for a feminized public ethics and as a narrative shape for describing the perverse and conflictful narratives which women themselves have made of their social and psychic relations to their own sex" (165). Perhaps what has to be recognized is the existence of aggression in all love relationships, a point that Otto Kernberg makes clear.

In answer to our question of whether one can be both feminist *and* Lacanian, Guyomard responds that Lacan is the one "who displaced the question of the woman, of femininity, from the impasse where Freud had enclosed her." What Lacan added to Freud was the question of feminine desire and feminine *jouissance*, with "feminine *jouissance* on the side of the infinite and masculine *jouissance* on the side of the finite and limited." Nonetheless, both sexes are connected to the two forms of *jouissance*, claims Guyomard. What Freud meant by the absence of the penis, says Guyomard, "is simply the perception of something that is different, missing, unknown, unmasterable in the mother's body or in a woman's body." Although this Lacanian reading replaces Freudian literalism, the reader still wonders why it is necessary for someone to perceive that something is "missing" in the woman's body, particularly if that someone is a woman? Perhaps it is because, as Chasseguet-Smirgel points out, focus on the absence of the phallus is less terrifying for men to deal with than is the power of the womb. Might it also be that, since the penis is not visible during the reproductive act (nor is paternity ever as tangible as maternity), there is an emphasis on phallic monism in the art and ritual of patriarchy—in compensation?

But Guyomard feels that, "like Freud, as well as in spite of him, a whole part of Lacan's advance follows the difficult acknowledgment of the weight of the Real, as he called it, of the difference of the sexes." A difference that many American analysts or at least feminists try to minimize. In contrast, it is not difference that we mind but rather the fact that difference is too often looked at from the point of view of the male only.

However, Guyomard feels that psychoanalysis can contribute to solving the problems of sexism and racism through the symbolization of differences, "the construct of a possible language in a place of difference" as an alternative to violence and exclusion, the two main ways by which humanity has previously tried to solve these problems. Like Kernberg, Guyomard believes that psychoanalysis can address the problems of the culture as well as of the individual.

François Roustang

In the published proceedings of a 1991 conference in Brazil, François Roustang claimed that analytic theory is "incapable of giving irrefutable proofs of universal propositions. Therefore in this sense, psychoanalysis is not able to nor should it pose as scientific" (166). Rather, Roustang sees psychoanalysis as an art that has the possibility of creating new forms, not in sound or matter but in human existence. "Every analysand is the artist or inventor of his own life." In his interview with us, Roustang claims that all he learned as an analyst he learned from women. Like Winnicott, whom he refers to, Roustang feels that there is a greater continuity between the life of language and the life of the instincts in women than in men. "What I mainly learned, thanks to women, in analysis, is that there are connections of an immediate order among human beings that are decisive for all relations, which at the same time are hardly perceived and are much less thought about by men." Most striking is Roustang's conclusion that "psychoanalysis is constructed entirely as a system of defense in order that this immediate relation not be apparent, and so one turns away from the essential question." Women, he feels, "are sensitive to many more elements and parameters that constitute a person or a discourse or a landscape...they don't need to master them to allow them to enter inside them." Are male psychoanalysts turning to women as sources of theory once again just as they did at the inception of psychoanalysis on the Freudian couch?

Roustang, a former Jesuit, speaks about women's ways of relating in terms that call to mind not only the American book *Women's Ways of Knowing* by psychologist Mary Field Belenky and colleagues, but also the practices of tribal cultures. His perceptions sound like Paula Gunn Allen's interpretation of a Keres Indian tale:

> Much of women's culture bears marked resemblance to tribal culture. The perceptual modes that women, even those of us who are literate, industrialized, and reared within masculinist academic traditions, habitually engage in more closely resemble inclusive-field perception than excluding foregound-background perceptions. (728)

Serge Lebovici

In our interview with Serge Lebovici, he is concerned with the phenomenon of prolonged *adolescence* in industrial society and advocates that analysts have "a reconstruction of adolescence, in the sense that one reconstructs the infancy of an analysand." Adolescence is not only interminable for the young, he claims, it is the new model for adults, who envy their children's sexual freedom and want to stay young forever. Atypically, he views the widespread incidence of anorexia and bulimia among female adolescents not as primarily psychological problems, for instance, as impairments in the mother/daughter relationship but rather as socio-cultural ones, the results of pressures in fashion to be thin conflicting with a superabundance of food. For Lebovici, unlike others, anorexia is closely related to the expression of sexuality. He speaks of it as "the orgasm of hunger." Far from wanting to destroy herself (here again Lebovici goes against the popular view), the anorexic wants to be stronger than anyone else by reaching an ideal of emptiness. In a sense, the anorexic craves the omnipotence of the androgyne.

Despite these problems, and in contrast to Roustang, Lebovici sees the transformation of the role of young women in society as more favorable than that of young men, men in France having lost their predictable pattern of development from military training to marriage and support of a family. Man can no longer be a hero in the old sense, for the old quest is gone. It is woman who now has a new quest—to find herself. We wonder if this change in developmental patterns will cause a restructuring of Oedipal theory since the Oedipal quest was above all an epic quest for men.

Even among the working classes the problems of men are being compounded. In such a group, a man doesn't have his narcissism gratified, whereas a woman who has children is constantly reinforced because she sees what she has produced. We wonder, however, if the changing role of the father will alter this, a role that most of the French analysts do not entirely approve of and that Kernberg sees as a temporary oscillation, at least as far as equality in child rearing is concerned.

Lebovici feels that psychoanalysts are now playing a big part in the treatment of infants since women often come to their appointments holding their babies in their arms. He also speaks of the considerable power that babies have over women. Like most analysts, he is against any utopian design for artificial reproduction outside the body but would allow for medically assisted procreation when necessary. Coitus and reproduction should remain linked whenever possible, he feels. "If one separates these, we will have a dangerous, deadly utopia."

As an older analyst, there may be some personal reason why Lebovici insists that "all babies are the children of the grandparents more than the parents." But what surprised us most was Lebovici's "astonishment" at not being asked about the problem of transference love. At the risk of being accused of denial the way Freud's Dora was, we must say that it was somewhat unexpected to find this kindly grandfather type fervidly recounting the danger for the male analyst with a woman patient. Rather than analytic neutrality, Lebovici stresses "all there is in men about the desire for conquest and for appropriation [that] can be realized in a love transference." There is a "sexual excitement that is much more perceptible in him than in the woman analyst...a desire to dominate." Nonetheless Lebovici feels that seduction is pervasive in life. According to him, daughters seduce fathers as well as the other way around. But above all it is the mother who seduces the baby into life, a point that Joyce McDougall had also made in an interview for our book *Women Analyze Women*.

Horacio Amigorena

As already mentioned, Amigorena believes that "analytic listening is marked sexually," that the differences between the sexes reveal themselves at the level of listening also. This is contrary, as he says, "to many very important analysts in the history of psychoanalysis who supported the idea that being a man or a woman wasn't important in being an analyst." He adds, "It is only with a woman analyst that a man is able to discover and elaborate on certain aspects of masculine identity," and no doubt he would say the reverse about women.

Amigorena notes that, traditionally, the differences between the sexes were defined by men as the fact of having or not having a penis. "More and more men realize that the difference is in the whole body, that the body of a woman is a body in which the connection to life is totally different from the body of a man."

Like Lebovici but more from the woman's point of view, Amigorena speaks of the seductive power of the analyst for the woman who may have never been listened to before in her life. "How is she not going to be seduced even if the analyst doesn't want to seduce her? Never will you find this subject treated in the psychoanalytic literature." This may be true in France, but Otto Kernberg has treated the problem of seduction at length in this country. Amigorena deplores the fact that women patients are often in analysis with a man for twenty or thirty years. They are actually in a great love relationship, he finds. And one day the analyst tells them that it is over, and they have nothing. He claims that he has never seen the opposite: a man who stays with a woman analyst for twenty years, and he suggests the importance of working with concepts, such as limit. "We should bring back the analytic work to what it was in its origins: a therapy to try to cure something. But analysis has become more and more a way of life, of love." Perhaps this is because love is in dire straits today. Might the analytic relationship be one of the last outposts of romantic love, paltry though this form may be? One might add that the relationship of male analyst to female patient is sometimes in danger of repeating the traditional cultural pattern of the tutor/lover and female innocent that is revealed in the epistolary genre, for example, the letters of Héloïse and Abélard, the feminine *Bildungsroman,* and more mundanely on college campuses. Amigorena speaks too of the woman's attempt to protect herself through *her* seduction of the analyst, although one suspects that this is far less of a danger to the analyst than the reverse situation is to the woman. Whether with a woman or a man, the analyst has great power. Amigorena finds that there is much on transference love in the French psychoanalytic literature but little on countertransference, partly because of the traditional stance that the psychoanalyst is neutral. But the analyst as a creature of desire is becoming increasingly recognized in French psychoanalysis, if only impressionistically.

In contrast to Roustang, for example, Amigorena is very positive about feminism, claiming that it has grasped new ways of being happy, not only for women but for men. For one, it has freed men by changing the customs of fatherhood.

Like many French (and other Latin) psychoanalysts, Amigorena stresses the great importance of literature over science in his formulations. For his psychoanalytic training, Proust was as important as Freud, Mallarmé as Lacan. When we asked him what he thought was the most important question for women in psychoanalysis today, he answered: "How to love a man without being trapped, without being subjected." This, he adds, is an important question that was "not very explicit before" but then he notes tellingly: "Maybe it was already a question for the hysteric."

René Major

René Major inhabits an eclectic place in France that contrasts with the rigid positions of some other analysts, a rigidity that has led critics to align psychoanalysis more with religious dogma than with scientific inquiry. As journalist Nicholas Wade has recently pointed out, however, scientists, contrary to popular belief, are often no more flexible: "People who have spent a lifetime constructing and defending a theory don't give it up because of a few mere counterexamples or contradictions" (*New York Times Magazine,* November 27, 1994, p. 40).

There is no doubt an emotional component that fuels both scientific and psychoanalytic allegiances. For Major, one of the most important tasks before psychoanalysis today is "to renew its language, which implies that it reconsider all the models it has used, those of biology, physics, mathematics, along with Lacan." This means that regressive tendencies have to be relinquished. "The problem is that students tend to rigidify, to fix thought, to want to conserve, to sacralize and dogmatize it. But the great thinkers are much freer, putting themselves more into question. They are always ready to reformulate what they have already formulated" (23). What Major says in this large, humane statement could be judiciously applied to most fields.

With regard to sexual difference, when we asked Major about feminine versus masculine desire, he answered that he did not know if one could differentiate between them "since one must abstract from this the foundation of psychoanalysis in psychic bisexuality." This statement suggests that men and women may be more alike (at least for some analysts) than is sometimes granted.

For Major, all love is narcissistic, and this leads to difficulties (if not impossibilities, we might add, if the statement is true), for "narcissism wants appropriation and it is always then that there are difficulties between people, for each person is many people, not just the possibility of a double" for the lover. No wonder that the quest for a soul mate has so often failed.

In speaking of feminine *jouissance*, that experience of sexual ecstasy that goes beyond phallic limits, Major claims that some men may have it also, a phenomenon that can be either pleasing or threatening to women. But whether the *jouissance* is the same or different, there can be narcissistic gratification for the woman, since the former provides a sense of mirroring while the latter offers a sense of completion.

Like many other French analysts we spoke to, both women and men, Major believes that parental equality in child rearing, suggested by Nancy Chodorow and Dorothy Dinnerstein in this country as a way of eliminating gender conflicts, would actually create more problems for the child: "Even if paternal authority in certain epochs has been a caricature," this enabled the child to "position itself, oppose itself, and find itself more easily."

Major believes there can be equality of the sexes without their doing the same things and even without changing the symbolic order. We cannot get rid of myth even if we try, asserts Major, because it is rooted in infantile fantasy. For him, the split between Madonna and whore is still very strong among men, partly because of the incest barrier. But this, he adds, does not mean that men are superior to women. If Major is right, we wonder if the prevalence of this splitting actually makes men inferior since it suspends them between love and desire, a schizophrenic way of life.

One of Major's attractions for us is that he writes compellingly about literature, avoiding the reductionism that too many analysts fall into when they go outside their field. In a way, what he does is "the reverse of the application of psychoanalysis to literature," for he tries to discover in literature answers to the questions that he asks in psychoanalysis.

Béla Grunberger
with Comments by Janine Chasseguet-Smirgel

One of the most striking aspects of our interview with Béla Grunberger was the presence of his wife, Janine Chasseguet-Smirgel. We had interviewed her for our book *Women Analyze Women*, which may have been one reason for her appearance, which we more than welcomed. But we wondered: Was she going to play Antigone to Grunberger's Oedipus or Antigone to his Freud? Would she be the explicator of Grunberger's text or his *aide mémoire*? Whatever else it was, this interview provided an intimate glimpse of a famous analyst couple *en famille*, interacting with love, affection, and some good-natured disagreement, combined with charm on the wife's part.

A major theme here is that of prenatal narcissism (one of Grunberger's original contributions to psychoanalytic theory) and its relation to the utopian impulse—the often dangerous attempt to recover this state of perfect bliss. Also stressed is Grunberger's emphasis on the positive aspects of narcissism and its function as a "locomotive" for the analytic cure.

In answer to our question of whether the early separation from the mother is also a sexual separation, Chasseguet-Smirgel notes that Grunberger disagrees with Robert Stoller: it is not just boys who have to break away from the mother to achieve a sexual identity. Girls also have to separate from her and to integrate their identification with the father. Grunberger holds that "the two sexes have to introject the paternal phallus to arrive at personal independence." As for penis envy, Grunberger believes that the desire to have a penis is a normal phase of feminine sexuality. A phase, of course, is not the same as a destiny.

As for the seeming preponderance of male perversions over female, Grunberger has a pertinent comment: "One can be perverse without showing it." Men's perversions tend to be anal and therefore obvious; women's are less obvious, as Louise Kaplan also points out in *Female Perversions*. A stimulating interchange occurs between husband and wife on the neglect of breasts as well as feminine cycles in the psychoanalytic literature. Grunberger denies that this is the case for him.

Grunberger believes that "analysis is carried out in a certain dimension of the psyche which is asexual. And in true love there is that also. That is, there is a narcissistic dimension which is asexual in itself." Grunberger disagrees that when one is in love, one projects all of one's narcissism on the object. But he does feel that love "has to do with prenatal regression." Furthermore, intense romantic love "is against life, and one has to explain it by death. One flings aside all the materiality of life." As for the suicide of the great literary lovers, such as Isolde and Juliet, Grunberger explains with quiet authority: "There is a way of being satisfied with one's narcissistic completion to the point that one cannot accept life as it is afterwards. And at that moment one might kill oneself, through narcissistic exaltation."

Despite her own striking contributions to psychoanalysis, which are increasingly admired, Chasseguet-Smirgel not only amplified points and raised objections, she had genuine questions for her husband. One sensed that she was there to learn as well as to interpret.

Otto Kernberg

What struck us most in our interviews with Otto Kernberg were his coherent formulations and his eclecticism, drawing as he does on earlier as well as contemporary analysts, both here and abroad. It is his knowledge of and inspiration from French analysts that mainly engages us here.

According to Kernberg, French psychoanalysts such as Janine Chasseguet-Smirgel and Joyce McDougall, André Green, Michel Fain, and Denise

Braunschweig, among others, have been "exploring the nature of the erotic much more systematically than analysts in other countries." To the French, Kernberg owes a key point of his object-relations theory: "Little boys become genitally free first, and are eventually able to establish an object relation in depth. Little girls have the opposite road."

Like most of the French analysts we interviewed, Kernberg does not believe that greater participation in child rearing by the father would fundamentally change the pre-Oedipal and Oedipal relations of parents to children and vice versa because unconscious identifications would remain the same. "We have to separate what look like revolutions on the surface from long-term changes."

Kernberg considers the splitting of the sexual object (popularly known as the Madonna/whore syndrome) as "practically a normal development in puberty and early adolescence in men." But unlike some French analysts who are less positive in this regard, he believes that it is usually overcome in late adolescence. Contrary to some other theorists as well, Kernberg finds "men as dependent, and striving with dependent impulses as women," and as capable of fusion.

But in contrast to some more optimistic thinkers in the United States, Kernberg does not believe that love can be divorced from aggression. On this point he is indebted to Georges Bataille's classifying of human relationships into ordinary work relations and "the ecstatic extremes of love and hate that disrupt daily life again and again."

In 1926, Karen Horney wrote that Freud's concepts of women were essentially the same as the little boy's: "The present analytical picture of feminine development (whether that picture be correct or not) differs in no case by a hair's breadth from the typical ideas that the boy has of the girl" (57). How much has this changed? Most if not all of the analysts we interviewed depart from Freud on penis envy and have quite original interpretations of the concept. Influenced by French analysts, such as Chasseguet-Smirgel, Kernberg believes that both sexes have an intense envy of the mother. This primary envy is then transformed into a secondary penis envy, particularly in narcissistic women.

Kernberg thinks that the early analysts who pointed to Freud's limitations because of his identification with patriarchal culture were feminists without the name. He also thinks that psychoanalysis has made important contributions to feminism by explaining the mutual fears and resentments of the sexes (he uses the term *genders*), "for example, the profound psychological fear of women against which paternalistic culture is a defense."

Unlike the idolizers and demonizers, the two groups that people often fall into with regard to Lacan, Kernberg gives a reasoned and balanced appraisal that takes into account both Lacan's strengths and his weaknesses. Kernberg speaks of the charisma, brilliance, and original contributions to theory, such as the conceptualization of the mirror stage and the Imaginary and Symbolic spheres that were part of Lacan's great influence. But Kernberg also considers Lacan's limitations: his mystification, the neglect of affect in his theory that the unconscious is structured like a language, and his slighting of the clinical aspects of psychoanalysis.

Lacan also has problems with the Oedipus complex. As Borch-Jacobsen writes, "the Lacanian Oedipus complex is not the actual Oedipus complex, but, rather, the Oedipus complex as it *should* be" (282), one that cannot exist in modern families. Lacanian psychoanalysis represents a longing for the old *pater familias*. We might say that traditional psychoanalysis in general is a theory of nostalgia, one meant to replace a dying religion. In *Civilization and its Discontents*, Freud asserted that we have to relinquish our infantile vision of God. We must also give up the childish view of the father. Possibly we hold on to it so tightly because it is even more difficult for us to give up our infant love for the mother. Unlike Lacan, but like some of Lacan's French critics, Kernberg feels that "the Symbolic is not simply a male-supported order, and reason and rationality are not simply given by the Oedipal father, but by the Oedipal couple."

Kernberg discusses the cultural differences that give rise to different psychoanalytic theories, the "optimistic environment-oriented form of Self psychology" in the United States, for example, as opposed to the more pessimistic, skeptical focus in other countries. What he would like is a combination of the American and French approach to psychoanalysis, one that would fuse empirical research and the methods of scientific research from boundary disciplines with the Latin emphasis on the analysis of the unconscious "as it emerges in clinical situations and can be applied to culture."

Kernberg sees psychoanalysis as a way of addressing the problems of the culture, provided it does not pretend that it has all the answers and engages in interdisciplinary research involving multiple fields, such as cultural anthropology, history, literature, and literary criticism along with the sciences.

Unlike many contemporary critics who see a sexist and elitist bias in psychoanalysis, Kernberg feels that it has universal relevance. Although he grants that the analyst must be aware of the clichés of his own culture, and should take into account cultural, ethnic, and racial differences in the analysand, he feels that we all share more commonalities than differences as human beings.

Psychoanalysis and Literature

Freud said that he learned all that he knew as an analyst from literature. Conversely, it was students of comparative literature and theorists of feminism who first turned to French psychoanalysis, for they found there a great interest in mythology, in philosophy, in the arts, as well as in sexual difference. To be sure, Freud had been a brilliant reader of works in multiple disciplines, but most American male analysts tended to be more clinical than critical, more practical than philosophical. There are exceptions, to be sure. Otto Kernberg is a major one. But in general, there is far less concern among French analysts than among American ones whether psychoanalysis is a science. It is almost as if for them it is an art, a branch of philosophy, a form of literary criticism, or even a subgenre of literary Romanticism, in which the themes of the tutor-lover, the woman as mirror, nostalgia, and longing that we find in the great Romantic poets and novelists are either accepted or put into question.

A book recently published in Paris (1994) by the famous if controversial publishing house called *des femmes* contains some of the papers given at a colloquium organized in 1990 by the Women's Studies Center (*le Centre d'études féminines*) of the University of Paris-VIII, perhaps the most avant-garde and experimental branch of the sprawling University of Paris system. The title of the book, like that of the colloquium, is *Lectures de la différence sexuelle* ("Readings on Sexual Difference"); therein lies the major difference between current French and American feminist (if not psychoanalytic) thought, for Americans would surely have called their book "Readings on Gender Differences." There are some exceptions, to be sure. For example, Drucilla Cornell, in this country, finds the term "gender" stultifying. "The demand for the recognition of the specificity of the feminine within sexual difference cannot appeal to what exists, to some core of female being, but must, instead, evoke what *cannot* exist under our current conceptualization of the juridical subject through the masculine ideal" (7). Or any subject, we might add. While gender-biased Americans believe that only the most striking reproductive differences are rooted in biology, and that all other variations in the sexes are culturally constructed and should be eliminated, the French are holding on tightly to their time-honored exhortation of *vive la différence* between the sexes. In the *des femmes* volume, Jacques Derrida, who has been having a dialogue with French psychoanalysis for years, writes that it still remains for us to interpret sexual difference, to decipher it; for it is problematic, mobile, not guaranteed.

In analyzing Pushkin's *Eugene Onegin*, that tale of love that misses because the time is not right—or so his interpretation goes—Derrida writes that there is no rendezvous without wrong moments, and no wrong moments without sexual difference—as if sexual difference itself were a history of wrong moments. When the heroine, Tatiana, wants Onegin, and writes her famous letter to him, she is a young girl, and he rejects her. Later, when she is married, he wants her. Derrida makes it sound as if the *Eugene Onegin* treatment of desire is universal, as if it is only the congruence of wrong moments that causes unhappiness. But in fact it is only because Tatiana is married that Onegin wants her, for she now mirrors and echoes the mother, the archetypal forbidden object. Any moment would have been wrong for him, a point that Freud makes with great clarity in his essay "A Special Type of Choice of Object Made by Men," which treats the inability of some men to choose a love object that is unattached. But is this distancing that is so typical of romantic love (a story of obstacle relations if ever there was one, at least in literary treatments) part of the male narrative, the male Oedipal journey that requires separation and distance from that first object of love, the mother?

Derrida finds that there is no reading of sexual difference apart from sex since it is always a she or a he that reads. It may be that, since French is a gender-inflected language, the French are particularly aware of sexual difference in ways that we are not. The French attribution of gender to non-sexed objects has often been dismissed as having neither affect nor effect. But an early piece by E. Pichon, "La Polarisation masculine-féminine," persuasively argued the opposite. The metaphor of sex invades the French language, he claims; masculinity is attributed to all nouns that are precise and methodical, and femininity to "everything that evokes fecundity without variety" (cited in Genette 366). Surely this unrelenting accompaniment of gender, this constant play of contrasting harmonies, must affect the French psyche in ways far more profound than gender-neutral English does. It is perhaps no wonder that the French emphasis on sexual difference is greater.

The Uses and Abuses of Metaphor

French and American psychoanalysts seem to have an almost oppositional view of metaphor. In his book *The Rhetorical Voice of Psychoanalysis: Displacement of Evidence by Theory*, Donald Spence claims that most psychoanalysts would like to give up metaphor (89) because they see it as interfering with clinical findings and the "banality" of truth, a banality that he favors. In contrast, the French see metaphor as a journey toward a truth that is constantly shifting and changing. A major reason for the difference is that most Anglo-Saxon analysts want to establish psychoanalysis as a science while those in Latin countries see it as an art in which myth, tragedy, and other forms of literature are encoded. (This is one reason why French theory has had more appeal to students of literature, philosophy, and art in the United States than it has to analysts and therapists.) Perhaps because theirs is the land of Shakespeare, some English psychoanalysts are also receptive to a psychoanalysis marked by metaphor. British analyst Adam Phillips writes, in *On Flirtation*: "For me, psychoanalysis has always been of a piece with various languages of literature—a kind of practical poetry." (xi). But such a statement would be rejected by most clinicians in the United States.

As women, however, we feel that a problem with the emphasis on metaphors in France has been the resistance to displacing them. There is, for example, what we are tempted to call the frozen phallus, a metaphor for the patriarchal symbolic order. As Susan Bordo writes:

> Poststructuralism has encouraged us to recognize that the body is not only materially acculturated (e.g., as it conforms to social norms and habitual practices of "femininity" and "masculinity"), but it is also mediated by language: by metaphors (e.g., microbes as "invading," egg as "waiting" for sperm) and semantical grids (e.g., binary oppositions such as male/female, inner/outer) that organize and animate our perception and experience. (167)

A major question that concerns us and that we posed to some of the analysts is whether the symbolic order or the metaphors that allude to it could be modified or changed. Alexander Marshack, in *The Roots of Civilization* (quoted by Lorber), suggests the richness that a female iconography could convey within a different worldview:

> Which *aspect* of the female process or myth is being depicted, symbolized, or given story? Is it the menstrual, the pubertal, the copulative, the pregnant, or the milk-giving? ... Is it the general image of the mother "goddess," the ancestress of the tribe? Or is it the female aspect which is related to birth and rebirth in all life and nature, and therefore, to a "female property"? Is it related to biological or seasonal cycles? Is the image related to the lunar cycle via the story of birth, death, and rebirth and by comparison between the lunar and the menstrual cycles? (283)

We recall the striking attempt at inscribing a new symbolic system by the artist Judy Chicago in her exhibition of a few years back called "The Dinner Party." It alluded to The Last Supper. But only women were present at Chicago's party. Each place setting represented a woman in her/story. Plates were designed to evoke genitalia, with the purpose of expressing individual women's creativity as well as sexuality throughout history and in different cultures.

The problem of giving women overt importance in the patriarchal symbolic order is not easily solved, however. As Lingis compellingly writes, in *Speculations after Freud*: "One was part of another body, one got born, weaned, castrated. Libidinal impulses are not wants and hungers but insatiable compulsions, sallies of desire which is desire for infinity, for *l'objet à*" (141). No wonder everyone, at least in advanced civilization, wants to escape the early pre-Oedipal mother, as much as we desire her. This has consequences in the public world.

Furthermore, François Roustang, in his interview with us, makes this observation about the primacy of the visual in men and ostensible desire for privacy in women in our culture (a preference for metonymy over metaphor?): "If there were a statue of a vulva on the Place de la Concorde or in Washington, I don't know if many women would tolerate it."

In contrast, however, analyst Monique David-Ménard speaks about the double order of the symbolic: maternal as well as paternal; in this country, Otto Kernberg feels similarly. The problem is that, for too many, the maternal symbolic order has been pushed down and functions as the repressed of the paternal symbolic order. We have to restore women's bodies as well as voices to culture.

The Bildungsroman and the Epic Quest

On the level of the individual (as opposed to the symbolic order, which of course is closely connected), perhaps Freudian theory fails for women not simply because it treats the primacy of the penis (a term used interchangeably with *phallus* in traditional psychoanalysis), but because it presents the same story as the male *Bildungsroman*, that of the boy who must separate from his mother to make his way in the world. In the end the woman is simply the reward for his achievement.

The Oedipus myth gave Freud the unconscious dimension of this male quest. Because the consequences of transgressing the incest and generational barriers, by killing the father and marrying the mother, would be too dire, the male child must set out on a search for a kingdom of his own, not his father's. One might say that the nineteenth-century *Bildungsroman* is simply a good example or confirmation of the psychological process that Freud outlined later. But it is more likely that this literary form, as well as the genres of epic and medieval quest that preceded it, provided part of the mythologico-narrative plot that contributed to Freud's theory along with the myth of Oedipus, seen only from the perspective of the son.

The female Oedipal stage, though little outlined by Freud—Jocasta and Antigone are absent from his account of the Oedipus tragedy—also has a basis in literary narrative. The girl too must break away from the mother, but she can do so only through a male intermediary. That is—or was—her *Bildungsroman*. Until recently, the main female quest has been for the knight who will rescue her, the prince who will awaken her, the husband whom she will live through vicariously. Contrary to some fairy-tale variants of this theme, in the female *Bildungsroman*, the heroine, though sometimes appearing to be passive, often actively pursues her savior, who, more often than not, disappoints her.

Current French readings of the female Oedipal drama present a "courageous" little girl who leaves the mother for the father, only to be abandoned by him. Too many female quest plots have followed this route or dead end of seduction and abandonment, abandonment after illicit sexuality. Much has been said about the splitting of the sexual object into Madonna/whore in the male psyche, a split whose source is posited in the prohibitions of the male Oedipal stage. Interestingly enough, the sources of this splitting lie in the female Oedipal phase as well. Not only does the little girl split the object of her love between the mother and the father; as a potential betrayer of the mother, she sees herself as split as well. In her future, unless she resolves this dualism, she has two possibilities: to be virginal and align herself with the good mother, or to be sexual and align herself with the femme fatale.

One question that some feminists raise is whether equal child rearing by father and mother, as suggested by Nancy Chodorow and Dorothy Dinnerstein in this country, would eliminate sexual differences in relation to the love object. Another we might raise is whether, as real-life narratives change and more women succeed in their quests for identity, irrespective of male intermediaries, theory will follow. Finally, we wonder what consequences the postmodernist concept of multiple selves replacing a unitary one will have on women's quest for identity.

Time, Space, and Poetry

The differentiated development of the little girl and little boy has literary as well as social consequences, not only in prose but in poetry as well.

Phillips, in *On Flirtation,* claims that there are three early relationships: to mother, to father, and to time. We would add a fourth one: to space. Because the little girl's relation to time and space is different from the little boy's, the sexes often grow up to have a different relation to the love object—and to literary forms and rhetorical figures as well. Although metaphor often presents rich and complex perspectives, it is also susceptible to abuse when it becomes fixed, or to banality when overused to the point of cliché. Furthermore, as Wayne Koestenbaum points out, albeit in admiration, metaphor may be plain wrong (*New York Times Magazine,* May 21, 1995, p. 47). It may be that critics have underplayed the figure of metonymy—the displacement of one object by another which is related to it or which is a part of it—in both women's consiousness and their writing. Women's greater concentration on touch, contiguity, and their de-idealization of the distant love object align them with metonymic discourse. Certainly the spatial closeness of metonymy, unlike the hierarchical distancing of metaphor (both in time and space), plays a large role in love poetry by women from the female troubadours *(trobairitz)* of the Middle Ages to contemporary poets, among whom Adrienne Rich is a major example. Nonetheless we have to admit that men's distancing of the love object in the Petrarchan tradition, for example, may not always involve reification as some feminist critics have suggested. "As with belief in a god, the durability of this object [the ideal] depends upon its distance," notes Phillips (*On Flirtation* 44). One question that we have to consider is whether women are more realistic about the love object and have more need for presence. Or is there another way to approach this apparent difference in women's and men's love poetry?

Freud himself insisted that women idealize less than men. Although the poets mentioned above do seem to fall into this category, there are others, as well as women on the psychoanalytic couch who idealize men inordinately, as Annie Reich pointed out. Might it be that women simply do not idealize from far away the way men do? Rather, they are able to idealize from close up. Why the difference? We believe that men's idealization is rooted primarily in their Oedipal stage, in the prohibition of the mother as a sexual object (not in the mirror stage, as has been suggested by Jan Montefiore). Since the father forbids the little boy from having the mother, he must keep the source of his idealization far away. Longing becomes a property of his love. Women's ability to idealize from close up may also go back to the Oedipal stage, in which their fathers are distant even though they are present. With the little girl, it is the father who says: You cannot have me. Yet there's more of a teasing, tantalizing quality with father and little girl than with mother and son because the culture frowns on the latter and approves the former. Because girls distance the mother, the first object of love, themselves, they are afraid of letting the male out of their grasp for fear that he will disappear altogether. Thus the spatial relation of the two sexes to the love object is different in the Oedipal stage, and this has consequences for their love life and love poetry later on. It may also be that women can idealize from close up because they desire fusion (despite their ambivalence, they retain a closeness to the early mother that they seek to duplicate in their romantic relationships) whereas men fear it. On this point we differ from Kernberg, who feels that men want fusion as much as women do. In contrast, it seems to us that the myth of Hermaphroditus that is recounted by Ovid, in which Salmacis wants to twine herself around the male forever while he fears being ennervated as a result, sums up some major differences between the sexes with regard to spatial closeness.

Does their double loss of both mother and father (as Phillips puts it) propel women toward metonymy, which, in the Lacanian view, represents the search for a lost object in other objects (displacement); rather than metaphor, which fuses two signifiers, revealing the latent meaning that they share (condensation)?

Luce Irigaray suggests another reason. For Irigaray the fact that women have two lips touching together instead of a penis is a crucial sexual difference that she feels influences aesthetics in fundamental ways that go beyond the gender-role differences brought about by child-rearing practices. According to Irigaray, a feminine syntax, unlike a masculine one, does not distinguish between subject and object, does not dwell on oneness or possession; rather it stresses "nearness and proximity" (Fuss 64). Furthermore, instead of favoring the substitutions of metaphor, it is happier with the contiguity of metonymy, that is, images of association.

Revisioning Mythology

As Judith Lorber writes, in *Paradoxes of Gender*, "Although myths in western culture have often repressed women's experiences or subverted them to men's uses, there is much subterranean symbolism that could be the core of a new cultural vocabulary" (115). Sometimes it is not even that subterranean. The myth merely requires a new reading, what feminist poet and critic Adrienne Rich calls "re-vision" or "the act of looking back, of seeing with fresh eyes, of entering an old text from a new critical direction" (167).

Unlike de Beauvoir, who called for the elimination of a mythology of women the way one might call for the elimination of poverty, Drucilla Cornell feels that "both myth and allegory are necessary, indeed unavoidable, in feminist theory if we are to seek a new economy of desire, beyond the logic of phallogocentrism, which has marked the very discourse of liberation, including that of feminism" (58-59).

Myth is the foundation for literature as well as psychoanalysis. It has been argued that it is not possible to consciously create new myths, something that many women writers and theorists would like to do. However, Freud not only revived the myth of Oedipus, he created his own psychoanalytic myth of the primitive father to explain the (male) psyche. Many feminists have denounced Freud's treatment of myth, particularly the Oedipal tragedy, as privileging the masculine at the expense of the feminine. In contrast, and perhaps surprisingly, Lacan privileges the feminine in his work *Le séminaire. Livre VII. L'éthique de la psychanalyse*, by giving Jocasta and Antigone primary place. In this work, Lacan idealizes Antigone for representing a "pure desire," which he sees as the ideal for the psychoanalyst. It is as if Lacan wanted the analyst to be born through parthenogenesis, through a virgin Antigone, an example of the male utopian impulse to control reproduction. There is in this claim of pure desire for the analyst an absolutism, which Lacan later abandoned. By 1964, he was writing about an Antigone who is born from a mother who is sexed and impure. As he puts it, "the desire of the mother [Jocasta] is the foundation of all structure ... but it is at the same time a criminal desire." Although women are placed at the center of Lacan's reading, Jocasta holds the position of incestuous and criminal seduction, and Antigone inherits it. Strangely unmarked by incestuous desire in this interpretation, Oedipus is at the mercy of his deadly mother.

Could the "criminal" Jocasta, who was merely a name in Freud's myth, actually be a displacement for the unsaid and the hidden in Freud's version: the seduction of the young Chrysippus by Laius, which brought about his death at the hands of his own son?

It is Lacan's shift from pure to impure in his treatment of Antigone that Patrick Guyomard analyzes and criticizes in his book, *La jouissance du tragique: Antigone, Lacan et le désir de l'analyste*, which he talks about in his second interview here. What we discovered is that it is not only women who are revisioning myth. Men are too.

But it is not enough to see women as the center of the Oedipus myth. Although women are primary in Lacan's reading, his version, in some ways, is as misogynistic as a reading in which women are totally absent. Myth is part of the Imaginary that becomes inscribed as Law. It structures the Symbolic and the subject. As Amigorena says, "Myth cannot be eliminated because it is myth that creates the subject." But what part of the myth should we look at, and how should we look at it? Lacan put Antigone on a pedestal but destroyed Jocasta in his own version of splitting the sexual object. Part of our journey in this book is to see how male analysts treat the woman as subject.

Note

Some of the themes in the "Introduction" are treated at greater length or in different form in Elaine Hoffman Baruch's *Women, Love, and Power: Literary and Psychoanalytic Perspectives.* See, in particular, the chapters "On Splitting the Sexual Object: Before and After Freud," in connection with the pervasive appearance of the Madonna/whore syndrome in men's psyche; "Romantic Narcissism: Freud and the Love O/Abject," on the similarities between Romantic literary themes and psychoanalytic theory; "He Speaks/She Speaks: Language in Some Medieval Love Literature," for some essential differences in women's and men's love poetry; "The Feminine *Bildungsroman*: Education through Marriage," in relation to the female quest motif and Oedipal stage; the chapters on utopia, which treat the male utopian impulse to control reproduction; and "Women and Love: Some Dying Myths," regarding the possibility of creating a new mythology.

Works Cited

Allen, Paula Gunn. In *Feminisms: An Anthology of Literary Theory and Criticism*. Eds. Robin R. Warhol and Diane Price Herndl. Rutgers: Rutgers University Press, 1991.

Baruch, Elaine Hoffman, and Lucienne J. Serrano. *Women Analyze Women: In France, England, and the United States*. New York: New York University Press, 1988.

Baruch, Elaine Hoffman. *Women, Love, and Power: Literary and Psychoanalytic Perspectives*. New York: New York University Press, 1991.

Beauvoir, Simone de. *The Second Sex* (1952). Trans. and ed. H.M. Parshley. New York: Vintage Books, 1989.

Belenky, Mary Field, *et al. Women's Ways of Knowing: The Development of Self, Voice, and Mind*. New York: Basic Books, 1986.

Benvenuto, Bice. *Concerning the Rites of Psychoanalysis Or the Villa of the Mysteries*. New York: Routledge, 1994.

Borch-Jacobsen, Mikkel. "The Oedipus Problem in Freud and Lacan." Trans. Douglas Brick. *Critical Inquiry*. Winter, 1994: 267-282.

Bordo, Susan. "Postmodern Subjects, Postmodern Bodies." *Feminist Studies*. Spring, 1992: 159-175.

Chasseguet-Smirgel, Janine. In Elaine Hoffman Baruch and Lucienne J. Serrano. *Women Analyze Women: In France, England, and the United States*. New York: New York University Press, 1988.

Chodorow, Nancy. *The Reproduction of Mothering: Psychoanalysis and the Sociology of Gender*. Berkeley: University of California Press, 1978.

Cornell, Drucilla. *Transformations*. New York: Routledge, 1993.

Derrida, Jacques. "Fourmis." In *Lectures de la différence sexuelle*. Paris: des femmes, 1994.

Devereux, Georges. *Essais d'ethnopsychiatrie générale*. Paris: Gallimard, 1970.

———. *De l'angoisse à la méthode dans les sciences du comportement*. Paris: Flammarion, 1982.

Dinnerstein, Dorothy. *The Mermaid and the Minotaur: Sexual Arrangements and Human Malaise*. New York: Harper and Row, 1976.

Freud, Sigmund. "A Special Type of Choice of Object Made by Men." In "Three Contributions to the Psychology of Love." *S.E.* 11:163-176.

———. "Civilization and Its Discontents." *S.E.* 21: 59-148.

———. "Femininity." *S.E.* 22:112-135.

Fuss, Diana. *Essentially Speaking: Feminism, Nature, and Difference.* New York: Routledge, 1989.

Genette, Gérard. "The Gender and Genre of Reverie." Trans. Thais E. Morgan. *Critical Inquiry.* Winter, 1994: 357-370.

Gilbert, Sandra M., and Susan Gubar. *No Man's Land: The Place of the Woman Writer in the Twentieth Century.* Vol. I, "The War of the Words." New Haven: Yale University Press, 1988.

Gilligan, Carol. *In a Different Voice: Psychological Theory and Women's Development.* Cambridge, Mass.: Harvard University Press, 1982.

Gilmore, David. *Manhood in the Making. Cultural Concepts of Masculinity.* New Haven: Yale University Press, 1990.

Guyomard, Patrick. *La jouissance du tragique: Antigone, Lacan et le désir de l'analyste.* Paris: Aubier, 1992.

Harrus-Revidi, Gisele. "La mythe de la séduction dans la littérature. Sa mise en lumière par la psychanalyse." *Psychanalyse à l'université* 14, no. 56: 81-100.

Horney, Karen. "The Flight from Womanhood: The Masculinity-Complex in Women as Viewed by Men and by Women" (1926). In *Feminine Psychology.* Ed. Harold Kelman. New York: W.W. Norton, 1967.

Kaplan, Cora. Review Essay. "Fictions of Feminism: Figuring the Material." *Feminist Studies.* Spring, 1994: 153-167.

Kaplan, Louise. *Female Perversions: The Temptations of Emma Bovary.* New York: Doubleday, 1991.

Kristeva, Julia. "Women's Time." In Toril Moi, ed. *The Kristeva Reader.* New York: Columbia University Press, 1986.

Lacan, Jacques. *Le séminaire. Livre VII. L'ethique de la psychanalyse* (1960-1964). Paris: Seuil, 1986.

Leclaire, Serge. *Démasquer le réel: Un essai sur l'objet en psychanalyse.* Paris: Seuil, 1983.

Lingis, Alphonso. "Lust." In *Speculations after Freud: Psychology, Philosophy, and Culture.* Eds. Sony Shandasani and Michael Munchow. New York: Routledge, 1994. pp. 133-149.

Lodge, David. *After Bakhtin: Essays on Fiction and Criticism.* New York: Routledge, 1990.

Lorber, Judith. *Paradoxes of Gender.* New Haven: Yale University Press, 1994.

Mitchell, Juliet and Jacqueline Rose, eds. *Jacques Lacan and the école freudienne.* New York: W.W. Norton, 1983.

Montefiore, Jan. *Feminism and Poetry: Language, Experience, Identity in Women's Writing.* London: Pandora, 1994.

Nathan, Toby. "De la 'fabrication' culturelle des enfants: Réflexions ethnopsychanalytiques sur la filiation et l'affiliation." In *Nouvelle revue d'ethnopsychiatrie* 17 (1991): 13-21.

———. "Vers une théorie de l'influence." In *Nouvelle revue d'ethnopsychiatrie* 22/23 (1993): 9-18.

Phillips, Adam. *On Flirtation.* Cambridge, Mass.: Harvard University Press, 1994.

———. *On Kissing, Tickling, and Being Bored.* Cambridge, Mass.: Harvard University Press, 1993.

Pleck, Joseph. "Men's Power with Women, Other Men and Society: A Men's Movement Analysis." In *The Gender Gap in Psychotherapy.* Eds. P.P. Rieker and E.H. Carmen. New York: Plenum Press, 1984.

Reich, Annie. "Narcissistic Object Choice in Women" (1953). In *Psychoanalytic Contributions.* New York: International Universities Press, 1973.

Rich, Adrienne. "When We Dead Awaken: Writing as Re-Vision" (1971). In *Adrienne Rich's Poetry and Prose.* Eds. Barbara Charlesworth Gelpi and Albert Gelpi. A Norton Critical Edition. New York: W.W. Norton, 1993.

Roustang, François. "*La psychanalyse: Identité et différence. Qu'est-ce qu'être psychanalyste?*" In *Esquisses psychanalytiques,* 1992: 161-167.

Spence, Donald. *The Rhetorical Voice of Psychoanalysis: Displacement of Evidence by Theory.* Cambridge, Mass.: Harvard University Press, 1994.

Winnicott, D.W. Psycho-Analytic Explorations. Cambridge, Mass.: Harvard University Press, 1989.

Wright, Elizabeth, ed. *Feminism and Psychoanalysis: A Critical Dictionary.* Oxford: Basil Blackwell, 1992.

one

Gérard Pommier

Why did you become an analyst?
This is a difficult question to answer quickly. I started my analysis because I needed it for reasons linked to the difficulties that I was having when I was eighteen or nineteen, and from that moment I also wanted to be an analyst.

What was your training?
I had a classical and medical training. I did my residency in psychiatry.

And your analytic training?
It was a traditional training for France. The school I was part of was Jacques Lacan's. I went through analysis for many years with another analyst, then with Lacan for several years. It was a very long training period for the followers of Lacan.

Where do you situate yourself in the French analytic movement?
The French analytic movement, as you know, is very spread out. There were many splits after Lacan's death. I was a direct disciple of Lacan. Therefore I

placed myself in that current. One might have many reservations now about how many Lacanian groups have a dogmatic conception of psychoanalysis. One could say that being a Lacanian is equivalent to having a rather sectarian position. But I accept the training that I received from Lacan.

Who are your patients? Do you have more women than men?
I think so. I am not sure. Early in the morning there are more men. In the evenings, more women.

Are the questions that women analysts raise in the psychoanalytic literature about women different from the questions that men analysts raise?
Whether they are men or women, everybody is interested in women. It is *the* subject of interest for both sexes. It is perhaps in the formulation of the questions that there are differences between men and women analysts. It is something to be looked at. But everybody loves women.

Therefore women are more interested in women than in men in psychoanalytic inquiry?
To the extent that the question of the feminine is in a way at the origin of psychoanalysis. I cannot say that I would definitively answer yes to the question of whether the feminine is the equivalent of hysteria. One might say that psychoanalysis was created by the hysterics who luckily were heard by Freud. But paradoxically, the questions posed by women in a way that led to the discovery of the unconscious were also paired with the exclusion of the feminine for the first thirty years following Freud's discovery. Therefore women allowed the discovery of the unconscious, but as women they were put outside the theory. The theory of the Oedipus complex only considered masculine development until approximately 1930. Until then the woman was considered in a symmetrical way to the man but as amputated with regard to him.

It is only beginning with 1930 that Freud has a conception of feminine sexuality that considers *jouissance* as something more than or different from masculine sexuality. Therefore there is this paradoxical situation in the Freudian field of discovery and exclusion. This is something very important to consider, for it has many consequences for psychoanalytic theory, and it is from there that today's interest in the question of the feminine stems.

Freud had very clear, apparently simple formulations on the question of feminine sexuality, but as soon as one starts commenting on these sentences in order to understand them more, there are few analysts who agree about their interpretation, even if they agree on the essentials of Freud's theory. There was in particular Joan Riviere's article on femininity as a masquerade, which is surely the most brilliant article, and gave me the most understanding of the Freudian position on femininity. And there is what Lacan developed on the formulations of sexuality, in his seminar called *Encore*, which is very important for the continuation of Freud's theory. That is, the woman is not totally in the order of phallic *jouissance*, which was the way Freud saw her until 1930.

How do you explain the paradox whereby Freud both discovered woman and excluded her?

I think that it is very important to acknowledge this. It cannot be explained extemporaneously. In fact the whole question is one of truth and knowledge since scientific rational knowledge is encoded in symbolism of the masculine order. The rational, the logos, is oriented toward phallic signification, which excludes feminine specificity. At the same time that there is the discovery of the unconscious which brings hysterics into analysis, there is a resistance to knowing what this means in terms of rationality since this rationality pertains to the logos and the masculine order. At the same time that there is an opening through the question and the plaint of the hysteric, there is also resistance to this knowledge. And this cannot be known at the very moment of the need to know. One can say that this connection between truth and knowledge is the very specificity of the analytic discourse in relation to science. Such a discourse is oriented toward the primary discovery of the unconscious, to the point that it is problematic whether psychoanalysis is a science because it has this kind of connection to truth. Therefore, there is this resistance to conceptualization that one might qualify without developing.

You said that everyone loves women. But the opposite is also true. The exaltation and denigration of women at the same time

are oppositions that are a problem for women.

It's true that everyone loves women. I didn't mean to say that it is a love without any second thoughts or that it could not eventually change into its opposite, but in any case even when love is addressed to what is alien to women, for example, among male homosexuals, they are totally obsessed by the question of woman and put her in the scene of their homosexuality, that is, in the place where women are most excluded. What is involved is the position of the woman as an object of universal interest, the specificity of woman as signifier of what is quasi mythical, to the point that it is also mythical to women. That's why I said that woman would interest everyone including women, for whom the woman is also a myth. And therefore they will also have this love for woman, which will be included even in their love for men. The presence of the feminine in love appears in the most rudimentary form of the Oedipus complex. This love can change into hatred at the moment that it is most violent. One might say that it is not exactly the feminine itself which is at the origin of this possible reversal. But it is love itself to the extent that it is an impossible passion that may be the passion of destruction to the extent that it cannot possess its object. Love in its narcissistic dimension, which is the one most described by the psychoanalysts, is suicidal. The love there is the love of Narcissus for his own reflection, for an appearance which escapes him. Therefore it can easily change either into aggression or into loss. Love is fundamentally bound to loss, to the impossibility of living through the body, and to replacing this discovery of one's own body with another body which is loved under these conditions, which are impossible to gratify.

You have written about violence in love. Do you think that women think about sexuality the same way that men do?

Not at all. I think that feminine sexual desire is structured in a very different way from the masculine sexual one for reasons which are easy enough to understand and which pertain to the structure of the Oedipus complex. If one considers the schematics of the Oedipus complex, the woman first loves her mother, then her father, to the extent that he frees her from what might be anxiety-producing and deadly in what seems absolute in maternal love. The fact that a father is there frees her from the anguish of maternal love, but the father is loved for a structural reason, because he has the phallus. Therefore the love for a man, the sexual desire for the man, comes to the extent that he is loved by the mother. From the beginning, sexual desire is impossible. It is stuck since this desire is directed toward a man only to the extent that there is a woman. In its own dynamics this sexual desire of the woman is paralyzed. It cannot exist without this paralysis. And if there were no masculine desire, which is totally different in its structure, feminine sexual desire would remain fixed in this passivity. What Freud described as feminine passivity is not at all the opposite of feminine activity. It is a specificity of desire which is the captive of its own process and development and which by itself doesn't lead anywhere. For example, a woman can remain for a long time without any sexual activity without that being pathological. She can live very well like that as long as there is no desire of a man which would lead her to other things. Masculine desire is not at all structured the same way.

You have written that the dark continent creates an impasse in *jouissance* for men as well as women. What impasse? Is this impasse different for men and for women? Is there also a *jouissance* envy among men? If so, is this envy parallel to penis envy? This is an interesting question. Yes, men are totally interested in feminine *jouissance,* for reasons that may eventually escape them, but that's not important since this *jouissance,* I think, allows them to exist. It's strange why that would interest them since they don't accept that *jouissance.* They don't know what it is and they cannot know it. However, they are interested in it. A great majority of them think only of that. That is due to the fact that feminine *jouissance* has a function which pertains to the oneness of the name (*nom*) and the no (*non*). That is, feminine *jouissance* reclaims a unique connection to the name of a man and even to the name of God. That's what there is in mystical *jouissance.* This uniqueness that is possible for a woman is something beyond the masculine phallic *jouissance.* Therefore a woman will pretend that a man is unique, that he is the most handsome, the strongest. It is that uniqueness which will allow her to accede to *jouissance.* It is not because the man is really more handsome or stronger—it is an extreme kindness of the woman to make the man unique—but in all cases that's what allows her access to the specificity of her *jouissance*. As for the man, the fact that there is someone who acts as if he is unique gives him a formidable presence, a means of access to his name, in his life, in his work, which he might not obtain otherwise. A woman may give him this condition for existence and for uniqueness, at least for her.

What about the homosexual man?
This question poses the problem of heterosexuality. If one reconsiders the scheme of the Oedipus complex, it is the father who frees the child from what is anxiety producing in maternal love. (This is true for both sexes.) Men will have this love for the father, for the phallus, and therefore the problem is how a man who goes through that will be able to reach heterosexuality, that is, to love a woman from a position which at the beginning is homosexual. That is something that we just saw in the question of the name because it is his name that the man tries to establish in his love for a woman. It is something that is linked again to the name of the father. The problem is to know to what extent the love of women is, for most men, fixated on something which is homosexual. Masculine heterosexuality is something very problematic, which is linked to this homosexual substructure. That's what Freud was saying in his *Three Essays* in 1903. What is more difficult to understand is not homosexuality but heterosexuality. That's what must be explained, for naturally the human being is homosexual rather than heterosexual. Freud was saying this at a time when it was very revolutionary.

In the United States, people wonder why Lacanian theory has been so successful since it is so phallocentric. Why do so many women accept this theory in spite of this phallocentrism?
I don't find Lacanian theory phallocentric. I think that it is Freudian in the sense that it supports the idea of the phallus as a unique symbol for the two sexes. This is simply from the point of view of what the unconscious reveals, for which there is no difference of sexes. It is that which is difficult to understand. Therefore one imagines that it is in connection with social problems that Freud, Lacan, and other Freudians have privileged the phallic symbol. But it is uniquely because of it that there is no difference of sex in the unconscious. Sexual difference is marked by the passive or the active

position, to be or to have the phallus. That could be demonstrated with clinical examples. Let us say that the place of the symptom is not in itself marked by the feminine or the masculine. It is difficult to understand because one cannot answer how this psychoanalytic position is related to social problems.

What is the connection between the phallus and the penis?
The phallus is a symbol; the penis is the organ.

But the phallus is closer to the penis than is the female organ.
It's difficult to understand; however, it is essential to speak about the question of phallocentrism. The phallus can be expressed in a thousand ways, for example, the whole body is able to represent the phallus, like the baby for a mother. Before being the penis it is the whole body. But to demonstrate this, it is necessary to analyze what castration is.

You have a very interesting definition of castration, which is both symbolic and psychological and not at all anatomical. But there is a problem here also. One might ask why you haven't used a word other than *castration.*
Because castration is unthinkable from the analytic point of view, there is no word for it. Freud used the term *castration* but not in the sense of sexual amputation or impotence, since, on the contrary, castration is what gives sexual potency. Therefore all the explanations that one might give of castration are besides the point because how can one understand that the infant desires the mother and is deprived of her, and that this is castration which, at the same time, gives the infant sexual potency? It's true that Freud could have used another term, but it might also be that the word *castration* is closer to the idea that one should try to express since there are clinical elements which are connected with the question of sexual amputation.

Could "castration" signify the separation between self and other, the other being the mother and the separation a sexual one?
Yes, but it's better to schematize. Freud developed all that into the Oedipus complex, which allowed him to transmit his theory.

However, the Oedipal stage comes after this first separation.
One must differentiate between the castration of death and the castration of
the subject, which is not the same thing. Acknowledging maternal castration might lead to denying this castration. That is, one might do anything
in order not to know about it. Therefore one should make distinctions
between the spirit of castration and the means of negating it. With all this
there are the elements of clinical psychoanalysis, the different forms of negation. Castration is expressed by different subjective positions: psychosis, neurosis, or perversion, according to the way castration is denied by the subject,
depending on the subject's answer to the pain of castration.

Is the mother always phallic?
I think so.

**She is phallic in the triangle, through her desire toward the
father?**
That's right. As the mother, she is always phallic up to the moment that she
reveals herself as desiring a man or men. But she desires no longer as a mother, but as a woman. The discovery of her castration occurs only when the
maternal position is put into question by the feminine one. It requires a lot of
attention to see how the maternal position is not in total harmony with the
feminine one. There is something here that is sometimes totally contradictory.

**Doesn't the mother have several phalluses? The one whereby she
is taken by the father's desire and the one of omnipotence: the
Virgin and Athena in their first archaic representation?**
Yes.

Is there a symbolic system which could replace the phallic one?
Replace the phallus? Why do that?

**There is a sort of mutilation of woman in the psychoanalytic
text. She appears without breasts, menstruation, pregnancy,
childbirth, menopause.**
That's true. Everything has to be done here. Psychoanalysis has hardly

begun, especially with feminine sexuality. There is no definitive Freudian text that allows us to consider the specificity of feminine sexual desire. And this is essential. There are a lot of little things, but it is not clear. It is not like the Oedipus complex where we know where we are. One might say that one hundred years after Freud's discovery there is the Oedipus complex and the castration complex. But the rest has to be worked on. Psychoanalysis is only beginning and is not finished, contrary to many people's belief.

What does penis envy mean according to Freud—and to you?
I can only say what I understand it to mean. The question of the penis can be considered in the sequence of what I said before. If one speaks about the development of love in the girl, which is first addressed to the mother, then the father, by freeing the child from what is anxiety producing in the love directed exclusively to the mother, is going to be loved. To that extent, the sexual love of the man's penis is bound to this first love of the father. That's a way of considering the Oedipal stage.

One can also consider love for the penis as something more narcisssistic. It's strange to speak about narcisssistic love as a consequence of a woman being desired by a man. But there is this oddity whereby, when a woman feels desired, the man has an erection. The erect penis is the equivalent of desire that is felt for her. She can love the penis for that kind of desire, can love the penis the way she loves herself. This is to consider the love of the penis through a narcissistic bias which is the love of the self.

Why not desire for the penis instead of envy?
This term should be verified in Freud's text.

According to you, is there penis envy?
I think so. It can be called that when it is something different from desire. There is a difference between desire and sexual desire. Desire is what propels human beings to act all their lives, to do a lot of things no matter what, or even to do nothing. This is different from sexual desire, which is totally sporadic, which occurs rarely or often, but in any case is very different from the desire to act. From this point of view, penis envy is very distinct from what may be called desire. The term *penis envy* is more appropriate to the extent

that one can say that we are dealing with wanting something the way one wants a piece of cake. When desire is much less specific in its object, the object of desire escapes. One can feel desire without knowing what this desire is aiming at. That can be ignored totally while penis envy is very specific.

There are many women, such as Simone de Beauvoir, who want a demystification of women, who want to ignore the mythology of women. Is it possible to eliminate the mythology of women? Why?

To denounce the eternal feminine, for example, which displaces woman, which puts her in the wrong place.
It's true. This provokes a displacement, which is an everyday event for many women; they feel that they are outside their own identity. But that assumes that we could be done with the myth of the feminine. It's a myth which has a function, and it seems to me very difficult to live with the exclusion of this function. To do so for women is approximately the same thing as atheism. Atheism is perhaps rationally desirable. But it remains that the exclusion of God has consequences which are sometimes totally destructive. One must also see if the exclusion of the myth of woman will not have even more serious consequences for women than the question of identity. In any event, it's a problem.

Could you speak more about the question of identity?
It's the same problem as that of the myth which was just posed. There is what cannot be named. The parallel that I was making between God and woman seems pertinent to me for introducing the problem of the absence of the identity of woman, which is not the same as nonexistence. God, for example, in Jewish culture can't be named, not because I don't want to say the name of God. I just said it. But because there is no possible definition of God. It is forbidden to name God.

It's the same for the signifier *woman*. All definitions that one might give of woman—it's not that. One cannot define woman by any single trait without falling into a specificity which belongs to the phallic order if one defines woman by her name. One might say, after all, that her name is the name of her father. One can take a certain number of traits like that, and one would not arrive at a specificity of the feminine. I am making this analogy with the signifier *God* because the fact that one cannot name God, that there is not any identity of God in the Old Testament, doesn't mean that God doesn't exist. On the contrary. This is a way of introducing this problem of feminine identity, which resists all the definitions that one might be able to give, which is something beyond and different from all the significations that one could give.

You have written that one doesn't become a woman; one becomes a woman again. Could you speak more about this?
I wrote about this becoming a woman again some years ago in connection with Freud's last writings on femininity. At first, Freud thought that there was a similar phallicism in the boy and the girl. That is to say, the girl, like the boy, was provided with the phallus at first through the love of the mother. And only in a second stage did the girl have to accept that she didn't have it and had to turn to the father to have it. This is Freud's classic theory. She had to become a woman. In the next stage of his theorization, there is a new period of phallicism for the boy as well as for the girl, for they are in a second stage in relation to the time when both had the maternal phallus. That is to say, they don't have it any more but are purely the object of maternal desire. They are within the maternal *jouissance*. It is to the extent that there is a supposition of a time before that one can understand the specificity of the feminine *jouissance* as something which goes back to that time, before the phallicism, which is also a return to maternal space in a certain way. When I speak about rebecoming a woman, this is a way of formulating Freud in a comprehensible way. What allows us to be sure of it is that this first femininity reveals itself in the psychosis of men as well as in women, where there is this impulse toward feminization. At certain moments of delirium, psychotic men might very well want to cut off their genital organs to feminize themselves. That is, they want to rebecome women in the psychosis. This proves the existence of this first mythical space.

We asked why the feminine sex should be considered castrated rather than different.
It is in a way the same answer. Until 1930, Freud considered the female sex as castrated in relation to men. One must say that many clinical aspects sup-

port this. A lot of female patients speak of their femininity in these terms. Therefore Freud had the best excuse to present things in this fashion. The thought of what is different, of heterosexuality, is what we can see germinating in the last part of Freud's work. It stops short at the difficulty I was referring to before, which is that heterosexuality is very problematic. To think about the difference of the feminine sex is problematic. Most human beings—here I don't say just men—both women and men, when they recognize their own difference, presuppose that other women are not in the same situation and that they might have a penis. This is strange to say, but there are feelings which allow us to say it, for example, a certain kind of shame at getting undressed in front of a man because they don't have a penis, and oddly, in fantasies, there is the presence of a woman who would have one. The feeling of feminine modesty depends very often on that.

Isn't this cultural?
I don't think so. Everything has been tried in societies. This is already behind us. Modesty resists all sorts of anticultural forces. Go to a nudist colony. No one looks at anyone else. One looks nowhere. They are wearing bathing suits over their eyes.

You wrote that the phallus gives a place of mastery to the woman.
The fact of being desired by a man takes the place of that which is missing to a woman. That means for this man this woman is at the place of the symbol of what is missing; that is, at the place of the only symbol. The only thing which has to be symbolized is what is missing. It is to this extent that a woman can symbolize the phallus as a symbol of what is missing. The fact that she is at the place of the phallus gives to the man his power, his strength, and for that she is loved or detested as well. It is this which creates the foundation of feminine power. There is no need for a woman to exhaust herself as do unfortunate men in different activities during the day. Women don't need to prove their power, which must be seen as a power which works with desire. A woman who walks in the street can very well feel invested with this phallic symbol simply because she is exposed to men's gaze. They look at her in a way which invests her with this symbol. But a force is also

a vulnerability because being at the place of what is missing is something terrible. What is missing is also the void. To submit to the desire of men is anxiety producing. That's why women walk so fast in the street.

What is the most important question in psychoanalysis today for women, about women?

It is the accommodation of what the feminine is. It seems that in the United States—I'm telling myself, "Be careful about what you are going to say. They are going to scratch your eyes out the next time you go to the States."

Why?

Because the feminine demands to be accommodated and to be put in the right place now. I saw a friend in New York who told me that to get a position in an American university, one should be either a woman or a homosexual or black, the best being all three at once. I want to say that there are important things that have been won by the feminist movement. It has gained a place which is fair. But why try to go into territory where the feminine has absolutely nothing to win? Into terrain which concerns what is problematic in sexual desire, in the encounter of the two desires, masculine and feminine? On this terrain feminism has absolutely nothing to say. Feminine desire is as entangled as masculine desire. One cannot say that it is machismo or phallocentrism which is responsible for the difficulties of feminine desire. There are problems of feminine desire and of masculine desire. On that level I don't think that feminism has to go to war. There is a deep discordance between the two sexes, which does not pertain to a social truth.

You are very far from the point of view that one often hears in the United States, where sometimes one might think that sexual difference could be negated.

It exists.

Selected Bibliography

Gérard Pommier has written extensively. However, his books have not yet been translated into English. We list here the ones that are pertinent to our subject.

L'exception féminine: essai sur les impasses de la jouissance. Paris: Point Hors Ligne, 1983.

Libido illimited, Freud apolitique? Paris: Point Hors Ligne, 1989.

L'ordre sexuel. Paris: Aubier, 1989.

Naissance et renaissance de l'écriture. Paris: Presses Universitaires de France, 1992.

——— two

Alain Didier-Weill

I would like to discuss the problem of femininity in relation to a seminar that I led in Paris, inspired by my clinical practice, that centered on the connection between *la parole* of women and *la parole* of men. I would also like to speak about silence. What is silence for a woman? Does she live silence in the same way that a man does? Independently of "be beautiful and shut up?" Where language places the feminine in relation to silence is something which preoccupied me very much with reference to men as well as to women.

I am thinking of something which a young woman told me in analysis. She was a prostitute who said something very striking about the meaning of the payment of money for prostitution. It was something that I found very profound. "What does a man pay for when he comes to see a woman like me?" She answered: "What he's paying for is the right to be quiet, that is, to make love without speaking." That made me think. It made me understand why, in general, we place the man on the side of bravery. He doesn't hesitate to give his life in single combat, fighting with a sword, or in the Westerns with guns for his honor. Why is it so easy for him to risk his life?

I think that a prostitute is in the position of an analyst with a man. I have a lot of respect for prostitutes. I think that they know what desire is. They know more than many analysts what they themselves want, and what a man seeks in them.

I want to try to examine why, in fact, a man has much more fear of losing his life when speaking in front of a woman than when in front of a gun. The question is: What does a woman to whom he has to speak represent for a man that is so terrifying that it puts him in a relation to death, not an objective but rather a subjective relation? On the other side one of my analysands—I learn everything from them—told me one time that the best thing she could receive from a man was wit, that is, language with *esprit*, unlike the prostitute who gets money, jewels, or other luxuries from a man and he is finished with her. With language one is not finished. A man who can transmit language ultimately can make her laugh.

Why is it ordinarily so important to be a man of wit but conversely to be silent with the prostitute? There are certain theoretical considerations that I want to examine here. There is something before analysis in the language, which has always positioned men and women through their symptoms, which are impotence for men and frigidity for women. On the men's side, power lies in the word, the sexual. Impotence or powerlessness for women consists of frigidity. From the start, language places the woman on the side of feelings, not on the side of words. Man is on the side of words, but words which can fail him. That is the most profound impotence.

Woman is on the side of feeling, and when I say *woman* I mean the feminine, which belongs to the man as well. It's a fact that a man who comes to analysis puts himself on the level of feelings when things went wrong, when the feelings invaded him so much that he could not act any more or have an erection or speak. It is a little similar with the woman. When a woman comes to analysis, it is always more or less because of the excess of affect, of feelings, and the problem she has in connection with speaking.

To go back to the crucial question: What is silence for "the feminine"? And what in that silence can be fatal for a man? Although one speaks about the femme fatale, one does not speak that much about the *homme fatal*. There is the *homme fatal* on the side of the romantic, the handsome moody figure. In fact it is the feminine in the man which is fatal for a woman, not the macho. It is the feminine in Don Juan which the woman cannot resist. However, what is fatal for a man is that, although his existence is linked to the fact that he speaks, he is reduced to silence by the famous mystery of the femme fatale. What is mysterious in her is not what she says, it is what emanates from her when he finds her fatal. The enigma of this famous mystery is what I am trying to explore.

Let us take one example among a thousand, the smile of the Mona Lisa. What is the source of the power through so many generations of this little smile of the Mona Lisa painted by Leonardo da Vinci? This smile interests me because it was to begin with Leonardo's femininity which revealed itself through it. It exemplifies what can disarm a man. A man facing an armed man is not disarmed. He is able to fight like a lion. But under the little smile of a woman like Mona Lisa, he is disarmed.

Why does a man in front of woman lose his bearing when he doesn't lose it in front of another man? First I would say that, in relation to another man, it is enough that the phallus be exhibited, phallus against phallus, a sign against another sign, to be sufficient. One does not need more. While under the silent look of a woman, showing the phallus is not enough. The man understands that the woman expects more from him. He has to demonstrate that this phallus hasn't simply been transmitted by his father but that he himself is the creator and author of the phallus. And that is what the *mot d'e-sprit* is all about. Because when a man is witty, he shows that he didn't receive the words passively but that he is able to create and innovate. It is in that way that he answers the question posed by the woman.

What is this question posed by the woman? And why can't she answer it? That's the basic question. What I think is that man is pushed back toward a certain impotence by the woman, and likewise the woman is herself placed in a certain type of impotence that the man can help her to get out of. They need to be together in order to make something out of this mutual impotence, which is not, however, the same for both.

Which question of a woman is answered when she hears a *mot d'esprit* from a man? What is given first, I would say, when it is satisfying, is a poetic creation, a creation destined for the woman because it is caused by her.

There is a question that the woman is asking herself that makes her suffer, that she has the power to ask a man from whom she expects the answer that she cannot give herself. Inversely, I would say that a man is a man when he is pushed to act because solicited by this question which he isn't able to pose to himself directly. Only the "feminine" can pose this question. That is to say that he needs the feminine to be put in the position of answering and by so doing, he creates the signifier.

Here I am dealing with the two fundamental signifiers that Lacan introduced when he reformulated Freudian theory into the famous groups of the S1/S2 signifiers. Let's say that the enigma of the feminine is linked to the appearance in the human of a knowledge which surges forth at a given moment, coming out of nothing. There is a knowledge which is deposited in the human, in the feminine, but it is a knowledge that doesn't speak. As Lacan said in one of his seminars, "a knowledge which says the truth but does not speak." (I was very receptive to Lacan at that time since I was in analysis with him.)

This is my hypothesis. There is a knowledge in the Real, which does not speak yet, which is antecedent to words, but which poses the question of truth. The problem is that knowledge reveals the truth without speaking. It is found in a receptacle. And man can receive this knowledge which is in the Other, the Other at the level of the emitter where the feminine is. I would locate the subject on the masculine side as the receiver of this knowledge in the Real that has been deposited in the Other. In such a way I interpret Lacan's formula where he proposes that the emitter receives from the receiver his own message in an inverted form. That is to say that the emitter is this silent place, the place of the Other where the message is emitted; one cannot hear this silent message with the ear. But it is heard in such a way that one has to answer. And it is as a speaking subject that one answers it; one interprets and answers the silent message. In a way one can say that the Other, at that moment, is in the place of emission, and will receive in return the message that it gave without knowing it. In the couple, I place the woman on the side of the emitter, the man on the side of the receiver, who receives from the feminine this message that he returns to her. The man does not know this. I think that the man is much more innocent than the woman. One has only to observe very young children, the subtlety of small girls who very early on know the truth about things compared to the awkward innocence of little boys who jump into things without knowing what they are about.

I am led to ask what type of suffering is there in the woman compared to the man? I would say that the woman suffers because she incarnates the question of knowledge of the Real which does not speak. What is a knowledge that doesn't speak, a knowledge that does not exist but that is? It is the difference between essence and existence. A knowledge that is and does not exist is not hallucination but approaches it. That is one of the reasons why Lacan was led to say, "La femme n'existe pas" (The Woman does not exist). What does that mean? That means that she is on the side of being, that the knowledge she presents is on the side of the Real, and that that is a knowledge that she cannot do anything about. Her proximity to this knowledge is such that she presents it to the world, in general to the other sex, because she needs the other sex. Since she incarnates such knowledge with such proximity she cannot receive it herself. She cannot at the same time both be it and receive it. You can observe that if this hypothesis is correct, the signifier that represents the feminine is in the Real, not yet in the Symbolic but awaiting it. There is a conflict between insistence on the Real and existence in the Symbolic, not a connection. There is a structural conflict, and no harmony. Tradition speaks about sexual harmony, but there is no harmony between the sexes.

A man who meets the femme fatale, this signifier in the Real, loses his control over language, babbles, as in comic films and cartoons. This is the effect that the sexual object is able to produce on a man. The wolf meets the ballerina and the eyes bulge out of his head; he cannot speak. He goes crazy. He is in a state of paralysis, where he is close to the psychotic who hallucinates. I am not saying that it is the same thing, but there is a connection. He encounters the Real. And when one does so, what is the fundamental thing that happens? Because it is not the Symbolic, one cannot treat the Real with the symbolic means which are in general at our disposal, that is, repression. One can neither repress nor negate nor deny it. That is to say that one cannot be an ostrich and hide one's head in the sand. That is why the man is shaken, a little like the psychotic who experiences hallucination. I don't say that he is psychotic, but he comes near to it. We are all brothers of the psychotic; that is to say that we are able to encounter the signifier in the Real. We are also all brothers of Hamlet. One does not consider Hamlet mad because he encounters a signifier in the Real that is a ghost. There is a connection between the ghost and the femme fatale which is what makes someone speechless. When he meets his father, Hamlet cannot speak. He listens. The whole tragedy is linked to the fact that he is plunged into inaction. I think that the commentators haven't sufficiently understood that seeing a ghost, that is to say, a signifier in the Real, plunges him into inaction. He cannot act except at the end, when he himself is touched by death.

I think that the femme fatale brings the man back to the feminine which is in him. One can call it homosexuality, and one can call homosexuality the feminine, the fatal within him, which pushes him toward the word, toward the urgency for words which is not yet speech, and is what Lacan called "this Real which says the truth but does not speak, does not exist." The nature of the woman's suffering on the couch is due to the fact that she incarnates the knowledge which one could say in Lacanian terms is the circle of the Real on the Symbolic. In Lacan's figure of the borromenean knots, it is the intersection that the Real establishes over the Symbolic. That is to say, the ascendancy of the Real over the Symbolic. Woman incarnates this knowledge in the Real, these two points of intersection by which the Real bars the Symbolic, where nonknowledge cuts the knowledge. And the suffering in the woman comes from the fact that she needs a man to make exist within her what does not exist, not a man who is going to pay, like the one who goes to see the prostitute, but a man who is capable of speaking, who is not terrified by the Real. Because finally, what terrifies the human being, the man as well as the woman, is the encounter with the Real. One has to say that all the nonsense in films, novels, Westerns that show us men putting their lives in danger in front of the Real, is a symbolic danger. They put life in question, but the terror becomes bigger when it is not their biological lives which are at stake but the life of words, that is to say, the symbolic life which is put into danger by the Real incarnated in the feminine knowledge or nonknowledge.

If I say that a man can lose his composure in front of a woman, it is, in fact, because he knows that a woman knows who he is. He doesn't know who he is, and in front of her he can only play the fool. In fact he knows that he cannot hide anything from her, especially in front of the one who is a femme fatale for him.

And who is he? What does who he is mean for a man? Fundamentally it is the connection he has with his phallus. Is the phallus directly transmitted by the father, or is there in the phallic metaphor a process through which the man has to give an accounting of the phallus? Is it that he does not receive the phallus automatically but rather has to create it all the time? It is what makes our job as analysts difficult; the desire of the analyst is not given to one forever. It has to be found and refound. It is not a state of permanent grace.

I think that Freud passed over something in femininity which he didn't understand when he spoke of feminine silence. He compared woman to the wild beast, the great criminal, the child, putting these on the side of feminine narcissism. I don't think he understood it all. Freud was not concerned with narcissism in the sense that he said but rather with the power that the woman has over a man, because she had a power that Freud could not explain, but a power that she suffered from herself, the power of incarnating knowledge in the Real, which made her at the same time all-powerful and powerless, all-powerful over the man, who is disarmed by this knowledge, and powerless because she cannot do anything about this knowledge if there is no one who symbolizes this knowledge in her, who makes something out of it and returns it to her. Words are the restitution for the hole of the Real that she represents.

I would now like to speak about the sexual relation. What is coitus? Lacan said that there is no sexual relation. To the extent that coitus exists, I would like to go on with some elements which are in the first part of our discussion to express in analytic terms how one might understand the exchange between a man and a woman as a commercial exchange. Commercial in the sacred sense of the term because I think that this commerce is connected to the original commerce invented by men in all cultures, from the beginning of time, in installing what one calls sacrifice, that is, the connection with the Other. The connection with the Other is fundamentally a commercial connection in the sense that each one gives something different. I was led to think that in the sexual relation, there is a commerce which lies at the origin of all commercial transactions that exist in a society, and which is the seed of all human activity of exchange.

I start with the following idea: the sexual relation is achieved through the erect phallus. When this erect phallus occurs, it doesn't come from the man. The man sees this phallus as a kind of strange body, which is not for him but for the partner, the woman. So what does this mean? We have to acknowledge an enigma: in the sexual relation the erect phallus is a signifier, taking place in the Real (of the man) for the woman. And that which receives the man is not a signifier but an encounter that is called the woman's body, which she does not give but rather is given. The man does not encounter a signifier but what is called the object in psychoanalysis. One gives the signifier; the other brings what is called the sexual object.

How can an exchange be understood between a signifier and an object?

The idea that supports this is that the sexual relation occurs after the event (aprés coup) of repression in which the man and the woman have both lost something, but not the same thing. What they have lost is not only the loss psychoanalysts speak of, it is something deeper. At a given moment there is a failure when the man discovers that the other does not give him what he needs: the symbolic Other. He discovers that there is a symbolic Other beyond the maternal. He is going to establish a symbolic contract, provided that first he recognizes the existence of this other Symbolic. He discovers himself as subject and is recognized by this Other, and the fact of being recognized as a subject brings him recognition of the Other. He will give to the Other, part of his body.

With reference to a man, what is called castration is not a pure and simple loss linked to a threat. There is a dimension of a gift which is associated with the threat. The dimension of gift occurs when he separates from a part of his body: his penis. This separation is interpreted by him as a gift which he gives to the Other. The problem is that the man feels that he is losing something symbolic. There is something that he negates in the Real by giving it, and that is what is called symbolic castration. There is a symbolic loss.

The woman does not lose from a symbolic point of view. Lacan spoke about deprivation. That means a real subtraction. She feels that she is losing something in the Real of her body. And the sexual relation must be an answer to that type of loss. This means that if the man loses from the symbolic point of view, something of the Real will come back to him under the form of an object because the object is part of the Real. And what the woman has lost from the point of view of the Real in her body will come back to her from a symbolic point of view under the form of a signifier which is a phallic signifier.

Thus you see that there is a commercial transaction between the Real and the Symbolic. It is a little like all commerce, the exchange of the object, of the Real with money, which is the Symbolic. Man brings to the woman something to symbolize the Real that she brings. Without this Real, the man would be like someone who has money in his pocket, which is literally money with no possibility of exchange between the Real and the Symbolic.

If the man brings to the woman the phallic signifier, this may explain why the woman, through the phallus that she receives, does not have the same *jouissance* that the man does. The man, recreating the phallus in the form of the Real, experiences something which has already been expressed by Aristotle, that man is sad after coitus. I think that one can understand this sadness because, in encountering the Other under the form of an object, he loses the Other, the dimension of the symbolic Other. In the case of the sexual relation—and not love—the woman incarnates a metonymy and not a metaphor of the Other. She is not then the muse who inspires the poet. She is completely different: the famous couple, the mother and the whore, the angel and the beast. And he is cut off from the Other by the sexual relation. I think that the depression after coitus is linked to that loss, to that separation from the great Other. It is the reverse for the woman insofar as she has the possibility of encountering a metaphor of the Other through the phallus. This gives her the possibility of having access to the great Other through the sexual relation. That is why Lacan—and it's not a real innovation—called this the feminine *jouissance*, a *jouissance* of the Other to which the man does not accede in the sexual relation.

I understand why one normally says that a woman sublimates less than a man, and it's not wrong. It's not because she has less capacity than a man—she has more—but she is able to encounter the Other through sexuality. And the man doesn't have this capacity. He loses it in sexuality. He is obliged to invent a longer and much more complex route to find the dimension of the presence of the Other which pushes him toward what is called sublimation. The woman in sexuality has access to something desexualized, while the man remains limited in and by the sexual object.

The virgin and the whore is the way in which the man splits the woman. The reason is that she is either the representation of the Other, the absolute Other, the unfindable Virgin, that he perceives essentially as a muse if he is a poet, writer, or artist. Or, on the other side, she is the whore who has to be substituted for that other signifier, or in the place of the signifier, substituting this object, this body, as cause of pleasure. We are not in the domain of language any more, of words. A prostitute noticed that a man came to see her and paid the price in order not to speak to her. As soon as the object is in play, there is no discourse. Except for small talk. What makes the man suffer, and the woman also, is the split that he is led to live between love and desire. The woman does not have this dissociation. The sexual act for her is something blended together through the intermediary of *jouissance*; desire and love are not dissociated.

Selected Bibliography

In addition to a forthcoming book on psychoanalytic research, Alain Didier-Weill has written many plays:

Pol
Les trois cases blanches
Le banc
Dionysos
La naissance de l'acteur
L'heure du thé chez les Pendleburry
Basse surveillance

In Press:
Où es-tu? Paris: Le Seuil, 1995.

—— three

Patrick Guyomard

What made you want to be a psychoanalyst?
It was a very old wish. I began my analysis at the age of twenty, and I wanted to study and also to pay for my analysis. From adolescence on, I wanted to be an analyst because of complex, personal reasons, certain impasses in my life, and suffering. It was absolutely necessary for me to speak. My studies interested me a great deal, but they were much more a means than an end. I was naturally oriented toward analysis. In analysis, there is always the risk of truth, as much in the words as in the listening. To be an analyst involves maintaining a connection to essential and risk-taking questions, with their unknown and enigmatic parts.

Who are your patients? Many analysts say they have more women than men.
Half, with a little bit more women. It is often said that psychoanalysis is the story of women. That's not true at all unless one considers the question of "femininity." The truth is that women and young girls are confronted very early, and probably in a way which leaves less space to denial, with what is

an irreversible change in their body. Young men lack this. Women are also much more lucid and more accepting of the idea of speaking. Men used to live and are still living with the idea of analysis as a failure or humiliation. They are no doubt menaced by it in a more grave fashion than are women, who accept the necessity of speaking more directly.

I also think that the confrontation of a woman with the question of maternity is so overwhelming and poses so many crucial problems that have to be resolved that women are more pushed toward the analytic process than are men, who can more readily put aside their problems and be less directly put into question by their progeny. Men are much more taken up by problems of work than are women, who, even though they work, are more conscious of the seriousness of procreation, the necessity of facing it, and at the same time the impossibility of facing it by themselves. There are more women in analysis than men, but it's rather a compliment to women, who feel the need to solve a problem more than men, who may blind themselves, put things aside until later, and isolate themselves from the problem.

What do women want and what do men want in analysis?
A man who is deeply depressed lives his depression as a catastrophe and prefers to take medication or adapt a willful or headstrong attitude with regard to his depressive, narcissistic, and regressive problems. A woman—and this doesn't mean that she will accept her depression better than a man—will live it in a very different way. Women need to speak more than men, maybe because they ask for more. There is also the relationship to death, which is not the same for men as for women. The coming of death, especially in its aspect of the finiteness of time irreversibly lost, of lost childhood, is lived in a very different way by women and men.

Men very often make demands at the level of desire, of sexual potency or impotence, that is, at the level of a life which is directed by a sense of success or failure. This seems to be specifically masculine. When a man's sexuality functions well enough—which doesn't mean a great deal with regard to basic problems—when there is no depression, there are many men who would absolutely not consider the idea of analysis. To put the problem in a symmetrical way, women do not demand sexual *jouissance*.

Even though that problem sometimes exists, it does not appear to be major or truly specific among women.

What is important is that their demand is more centered on maternity, on whether they want children or they don't want them. It's an enormous question.

They don't expect from analysis what men expect from it. For women it is more on the level of *how to live* with a certain number of difficulties. In all analysis there is a connection to childhood which is not the same for a man as for a woman. There is much more the sense of a lost childhood in a woman than in a man. What adolescence may have represented as a passage and a change is also revealed in two ways: the aspect of what is no longer there and also what is still there, of what has been lost and of what continues. In a man there is much more of a false sense of continuity. This comes from the body. A woman is transformed in her body from the moment of puberty, when she must think about, understand, reflect on, and measure a passage, a change. She becomes another, violently assaulted by sexuality, by the desire of men, and the change in her image, the change also in the way others look at her, and the way that she looks at herself. An adolescent girl can measure the change between what she was, what she is no longer, and what she is becoming. With an adolescent boy there is on the contrary a sense of false continuity. There isn't the same sense of rupture, or rather the rupture is of another mode.

In the relationship between the sexes, do you see a terror expressed by men with regard to women?
In men there is a manifest terror of women, particularly of mothers. Terror which is bound to maternal omnipotence, which is a real fact of childhood. In infancy the power of the mother is not at all similar to the power of the father. The terror of the mother is proportional to what she is able to give and to what the infant is able to demand of her. One is necessarily more afraid of someone that one expects a lot from or who has given a lot than of someone from whom one expects nothing, and who has given little. It is from this perspective that we have to see this omnipotence.

What men call the power of women, of mothers, is their own dependency in relation to women, the mothers. Sexually, in a man, the fear of a woman is proportional to the desire of a man for that woman, and also to the way a man may feel himself overcome, anguished by the violence of this desire, the impossibility of facing it, mastering, or controlling it. Therefore what is projected onto the other at the level of omnipotence is very often the perception that the desire aroused by another in a man *doesn't belong to him*. This strangeness that desire provokes in every human being, this desire is truly one of the names of otherness. That is to say, the physical drive and psychic presence of another dimension, which escapes him in that he cannot control it, is projected very logically onto the fear of the Other, the other sex, which becomes the cause of desire that the man feels in himself.

What Freud was able to say about the mystery of desire in women—what do women want?—this dark continent, about the awareness of sexual difference, or, to use his own terms, the perception of the absence of the penis in the woman, does not have to stem from a visual or perceptual phenomenon. For a boy as well as for a girl, it is simply the perception of something which is different, missing, unknown, unmasterable in the mother's body or in a woman's body which posits the question of desire in the mother, of her *jouissance* in a nonsymmetrical and mysterious relationship. All that we can say on the level of the visible, of representation, or of nonrepresentation is that these images of this primary fact are simply those of the alterity of the mother. All that men were able to exert as violence and repression against women and against mothers in the history of humanity, repression in which mothers were accomplices, has always aimed at mastering this part of the unknown which could represent women's desire. For from the moment that something is unknown, it has to be completely dominated.

How do you explain this complicity of women?
There is a complicity when things go well between mothers and sons. Freud used to say that it was the most satisfying relationship. I don't know if it *is* to the point that he thought, but this is not totally false. There is also the problem of the relation among women, the rivalry among them, among mothers. What one sees in the mother/daughter relationship is so destructive, dangerous, menacing that finally switching over to men may give the feeling of total security. One of the problems of current feminism seems to me whether women can trust other women. One can only hope so. The

question is open, but the trust among women is not that evident, especially when there are men and children at stake.

I see women in analysis who call themselves feminist, who sometimes are at the boundary of a certain homosexuality. These are interesting but complex analyses, with this special difficulty: in the transference there is a whole dimension of violence against men, of incomprehension of men, which centers on the repressive aspect of a certain function of paternity. These women think that men do not understand anything about women either.

Some think that it is important in an analysis that the analyst understands the patient; this is not at all certain. At the beginning of my practice I tried to understand my patients. Lacan told me and I realized that it was a mistake. It is a mistake to understand and to want to understand. There is a certain ambiguity in the word *understand* (*comprendre*). Not to try to understand does not mean that one isn't human, sensitive, and compassionate. But if understanding means to take someone's place, to be able to live what that person is living, to project onto him or her, to structure a relation of words around the idea that one can put oneself in the place of the other, then this is a total mistake in connection to analysis. Great progress is made from the moment when someone realizes that he is able to speak to an analyst who hears him but who doesn't try to understand, that is, who doesn't try at all to put himself in his place any more than the analysand tries to put himself in the place of the analyst. Talking only becomes possible in a place of listening and alterity, in which the Other is always the unconscious placed beyond comprehension.

In analysis with these women, there is a moment when it seems that the person who counts the most in their lives, the one with whom they had the most investment, the most passion, is evidently the mother, and that is truly their sorrow. What couldn't be settled between their mothers and them—and here I am thinking of a very special patient whose mother died at the moment of the daughter's adolescence—no one can cure; nothing will come to replace what their mothers couldn't give them and also what they feel they couldn't give their mothers.

In their analysis there always comes a moment when the question of dealing with a male analyst is raised. I try to recognize the limits of my position. In an analysis it is not necessary to try to negate one's own limits; on the contrary. It is much more in being oneself, in thinking and working from the most restrictive, acute determinations and strongest limitations that one is able to do something, not in negating them. Good dancers are those who do something with their body as it is and not those who try to project themselves into a body that they don't have.

If women desire at a given moment to have an analysis with a woman, to speak with a woman, that is all right. I recognize the strength of their investment in the maternal question and their need to go back to a place which is manifestly the most important for them. Often enough they prefer to speak to a man who has his own resistances rather than to a woman who is supposed to understand them much more, but with whom the risks of fusion, of passion, and also of failure would be much more dramatic. The repeated failure with a woman analyst for this type of patient is lived as a drama so that finally such patients prefer the risk of speaking to a man with much more distance. The reason is that there is too much suffering in their relation with their own mother, an impossiblity of talking, of giving their mother what they would have liked to give her; and I think that one must go further: the impossibility of making the mother speak, of receiving words of truth from her.

Quite often one realizes that children do not ask their parents, their mothers, for a solution or an idealization of life, or that everything be fixed up. Children realize very quickly that there is something that cannot be cured in the suffering of a parent. But they expect the word of truth, that is, that someone say simply what happened or didn't in life, what to expect or not, but in any case a word. In some of these women, there was the impossibility of receiving from their mother the word of truth about her suffering, her story, her life. In children who feel all-powerful, the consequence is that if the mothers couldn't speak, it was because of the daughters. As little girls they really thought that if they couldn't establish contact with their mothers, it was because they weren't good enough, strong enough, able enough; they didn't succeed enough in school, or they were not boys. From the failure of this relationship, they got a feeling of contempt toward women, which is above all a feeling of contempt toward themselves.

Very often it is women who enter analysis with an extraordinary feeling of self-contempt. When a woman feels this way about herself, it is evident that to undertake an analysis with a woman is much more dangerous. She is haunted by this contempt and thinks that she will never make it. At least with a man, there is a mimimal possibility of hate, of violence, of alterity, which is a little bit more narcissistic and finally more rewarding than a transference with a woman, which is more dangerous. For certain women, hatred and violence against a man are more livable because they are accepted perhaps as being truer in the strangeness of the difference of the sexes. In the abyss of this difference, such feelings are more acceptable than they are toward someone of the same sex, where they become intolerable. With someone so close, how can one have so much strangeness, difference, otherness, and even contempt and hatred?

In a relation where the difference of the sexes is marked, this difference allows one to symbolize, at the price of a certain loss, another difference just as radical, which is the extreme solitude in which the human being is found. Between each human being and his or her origins, there is at the same time a continuity, a transmission, a filiation, a symbolization, and a radical exclusion which makes each one who comes into the world have to die and be totally excluded from where he or she comes from. It is in this conglomeration of problems that one has to pose the question of the difference of the sexes.

A patient was telling me—and I don't know if she will see a woman analyst some day—that she realized that she preferred for the moment, and in spite of everything, to speak to a man because at least with a man there is that element of resistance. This resistance, as she said, is like a wall: one can lean on it.

Analysis proceeds by the lifting of resistances, but at the same time, the resistance exists by the mere fact of the unconscious. The idea of lifting all repression, suppressing all resistance, is something totally impossible without the analytic process. If one leans on nothing, one cannot hold on. Lacan called this, *"je n'en veux rien savoir"* ("I want to know nothing about it").

The question of racism has a great connection to the one of sexual difference. The psychic roots of racism are linked to the question of sexual identity, to everything that plays into the relationship man/woman. The way analysis is able to prevent racism or sexism from continuing is to make understood that its work is in great part the work of the symbolization of differences. That means the construct of a possible language in a place of difference. This is the alternative that psychoanalysis can offer to the way that humanity has tried to resolve these problems up till now, that is, through the procedures of exclusion.

One can see that humanity has always invented "therapeutic" procedures whereby societies, families, communities, clans, tribes, tended to regulate the problem of what could not be assimilated. But they always resolved it by massacre, war, exclusion, racism, sexism, oppression, by an extremely rigid codification of the sexual difference, of the roles of the one and the roles of the Other. The value of psychoanalysis—and this must remain present in the minds of psychoanalysts, even though neither Freud nor psychoanalysis was able to stop the rise of Nazism—and the goal of psychoanalysis must be to remain civilizing, to offer alternatives of recognition to the human being for problems of differences in general and the problem of otherness besides the means of exclusion which have always been used.

You don't seem to have any problem using the word *feminism*, which is rejected by some women as being simply another *ism* in the system.
In France, there is also the word *féminitude*, which is used in a different sense. Feminism seems to be too symmetrical a term in a culture marked by the masculine, and when women do not want to substitute one oppression for another, one system by another, when they don't want to place themselves in a symmetrical trap, they reject the word *feminism*. (And it is in this sense that Lacan says that "The Woman" does not exist.) The word *feminism* does not bother me. I think it is important that women think, fight, work for their own voice, their own condition, for the good reason that if they don't do it, no one will do it for them. On the other hand, there is a lot to win. And from this point of view, independently of what might be called excessive or problematic, why won't we use the term *feminism*? That it causes problems to children and to men is undeniable, but these are the problems of men. It is up to men to face them and to speak about them with women.

What problems might feminism bring to men?
The essential problem posed to men is the problem raised from the beginning of feminism but heard about very little because more urgent political

problems on the level of women's social conditions and the rights of young people were making themselves felt. There is no change if the change is not inscribed in law. In spite of patriarchal oppression, true oppression, of which women speak, it remains true that mothers were partially accomplices of this oppression for reasons that I do not pretend to analyze totally, but among which remains the extreme difficulty that relations among women may constitute. To avoid all these problems of violence, rivalry, all that is potentially destructive and also important in the mother/daughter relationship, a lot of women find in their sons and in their husbands a kind of mediation. If there is a change, it must also come from the mothers. Even in patriarchy the power of mothers was already present.

The problem that arises is that of the power of women, which has always been in part as great as men's. Men are going to find themselves confronted socially by a threat and a redefinition of their own identity when this question of the power of women won't be simply a fantasy but must exert itself in reality: women with skills, responsibilities, political power will bring a profound redefinition of paternal and masculine identity.

One of the reasons why paternal power was violently installed, and the identity of the father so protected symbolically in societies, in the laws, was because at the level of the father's identity there was something potentially fragile for a man. Paternal identity belongs more to the Symbolic than the Real whereas a mother is sure that the child comes from her. It is that which even makes her delirious at some moments: she wonders how another human being could come out of her body. But on the level of identity, there is a tenuousness which gives the father the impression of being only a kind of insect, having merely a seminal role in copulation; aside from that, he feels totally useless, superfluous, and that one can do very well without him, and this is sometimes not so false. That is why men constructed a whole symbolic system which besides being violent is coherent, and assures the identity of each one, especially the position of the father and of the son. And this is at the price of a certain place given to the identity of women who become objects of exchange, and to the extent that they aren't mothers or potentially mothers they see their place reduced to almost nothing.

From the moment that all this changes, men become much more fragile. In all the problems of the new techniques of reproduction, one sees very well that the real question is: What is a mother? But the question on the legal level is also: What is a father? This brings a redefinition of the term *father*, which in order to be coherent implies a redefinition on the legal level, an inscription, and a reflection of society. I think that the father's identity has to be given by the social order, probably much more than the mother's identity.

Formerly there was an extreme constraint for women, which put into question their being, their identity, if they were not mothers. A woman who didn't have a child, a son, could be repudiated, rejected, abandoned. I think that what women won through their struggle was the power to be women without being biological mothers. That is something essential. But on the men's side, there is around the notion of father, something very indeterminate.

Can one be both feminist and Lacanian?

That is a question to ask women. Some think yes and some think no. There is a difficulty which stems from what one means by Lacanian. Lacan is, I think, the one who displaced the question of the woman, of femininity, from the impasse where Freud had inclosed her. He showed that in all that Freud was describing as men's fantasy of a woman or of a phallic mother, the real question raised was that of desire: the woman's desire. He also showed that what one calls the phallus, the fantasmatic phallus in infancy, that is, in the psychic economy, is not an object that men are provided with and women are missing, but rather that of the signifier of desire. Consequently, the psychoanalytic question—psychoanalysis did not invent the phallus (all myths and all cultures contain representations of the phallus as a sexual organ)—is that of the symbolization of desire. The two sexes, men as well as women, have a connection to the phallus, if one means by phallus the signifier of desire, that is, the signifier of lack, which affects every human being from the moment that he/she speaks. There is only desire and recognition of desire with the dimension of lack. From this point of view, to take things too biologically, too concretely, or too much on the level of the image is as mistaken for men as for women. If one thinks that a woman doesn't have the phallus and is therefore missing everything, and that a man has the phallus and consequently lacks nothing, this is totally false.

Lacan brought something which is really irreversible on this point, that is, to show that desire is centered on the phallus and that the question of castration, which is the fundamental lack in its connection to law, is as relevant to men as to women. The relation to lack affects both sexes. From this point of view one can only be Lacanian. And I even think that in France, a certain number of feminists not only refer to Lacan but have seen in Lacan's assertions a recognition of the question of desire in its true place.

Besides all this, there are a certain number of questions, which are difficult to analyze in detail, concerning women and mothers that Lacan didn't approach. All theory is limited. Then, there is the "phallic" use that is made of Lacan, whereby the theory, in all that it represents as systematic and powerful, becomes an imaginary phallus, that is, becomes the object which is possessed by men *and* women in order not to raise questions any more and to believe that the problem of sexual desire is resolved and above all that one knows what men and women desire. From the point of view of the political use of Lacanian theory, it is in a way difficult to be Lacanian and feminist if one thinks that being a feminist presupposes that women are in a place where speech can reveal freedom and truth in a very different way from men's discourse.

Would you speak about feminine *jouissance* compared with masculine *jouissance*?

On this question of *jouissance*, Lacan also said things that are important and right, for example, in putting feminine *jouissance* on the side of the infinite and masculine *jouissance* on the side of the finite and limited. However, in Lacan as in Freud, the question of the masculine and the feminine is not always simple because there is at the same time the reality of the body (there is no *jouissance* if there is no body). But at the same time, men and women do not divide simply according to the reality of the body. Every man is connected to the infinite, and every woman is also connected to masculine *jouissance*, to castration, to what is limited. Lacan called this connection to the infinite, to a nonlimited *jouissance*, feminine in his terms. And maybe there he recognized more than Freud the positive aspect of a space, of a place of speech, identifying it sometimes with the unconscious that Freud had recognized but to which he gave the name of dark continent.

What seems important to me is what the connection to *jouissance* represents, that is, of the feminine or the nonfeminine and the place occupied by the analyst. To use an expression of Lacan, the analytic place—"that feminizes." What does that mean? It connects to the unconscious, to the infinite of *jouissance*, to castration, but also to passivity, which is very specific. Some analysts, for example, Dolto, think—and Lacan thought so also—that it is much more natural for a woman than for a man to be an analyst. Lacan used to say that women analysts were analysts naturally and without knowing it. They knew it almost from birth, one might say. Whereas for a man, there is a sort of violence, of modification, of change, which of course has something to do with his own feminine identifications, his relationship to his mother, but there is also something which puts into play his sexual identity in a very different way from that of a woman.

In the man/woman relation, that is an extremely important question to raise. For Freud, the birth of analysis consisted in identifying with hysteria and at the same time pulling something out from it, that is, locating and recognizing what was at stake in feminine hysteria and, at the same time, situating himself as a man in relation to this hysteria. What happened to Lacan is similar. The historic function of Lacan in psychoanalysis was to reintroduce the function of the father and therefore a certain symbolic function at a time when psychoanalysis was dominated by three awesome women: Anna Freud, Marie Bonaparte, and Lampl de Groot—leaving aside Melanie Klein. It was a moment when psychoanalysis risked becoming a women's field.

There is a danger for psychoanalysis and for women that psychoanalysis periodically becomes a domain of women and children. The question of sexual difference and paternity might be put aside (when one puts something aside, there is always something else which takes its place) for the benefit of the mother/child relation. This might then appear very naturally as the model for the human being in connection to language and to a place which is out of reach. The fantasmatic mother constitutes the place where one hopes to find all the answers, that is, a kind of reestablishment of maternal omnipotence, which not only installs and reinstalls an all-powerful mother not marked by the question of the father, by castration, but who at the same time, little by little, risks retransforming her analysands into little children before the moment when the question of sexual difference was posed. That is, a moment when they are sort of undifferentiated babies, for whom it is more important to be the mother's infant than the mother's son or daughter. Like many other social professions that deal with childhood, for example, teaching, there is a way of thinking that holds that psychoanalysis should be performed mainly by women. That would mean that something maternal takes over; at the same time there would be a kind of subterranean disqualification of the psychoanalytic function. In France, seventy-five percent of the teachers are women. This has resulted in putting down the profession, which reveals itself on the social level in the reality of salaries. We are dealing here with the weight of the social order. Psychoanalysis is in a way threatened by the same danger, forgetting that it is not only dealing with the maternal. It concerns desire, that is, the connection with the other sex, with the relation to the mother and to the father. It concerns the question of death, of *jouissance*, of madness, and certainly the maternal, but not only the maternal.

In his historic function of returning to Freud, Lacan reemphasized the danger of maternalization in psychoanalysis. This corresponded to a totally different position in psychoanalytic thinking. Today we are still feeling the effect of this legacy, but I think that the danger remains. What is absolutely important for male analysts to know—and this is a question of discourse, it's not simply a question of individual analysis—is that the position of the analyst feminizes.

There is another problem for a male analyst when he analyzes women: the envy of women and what that represents for a man. There is a whole aspect of male fantasies that Melanie Klein has revealed—although I don't think that they are as symmetrical as she puts it. Penis envy might be the envy that the little boy or the little girl feels for the mother; and the envy of a man for the mother is the envy of her maternity, of this power that she has in her body that a man does not have and the envy also of a mother's possible familiarity with the unconscious and ability to decode it, of her understanding the children and knowing what to do. There are all these dimensions. Very often for some men who become analysts, there is unconscious envy, and here I use the term *envy* in the Kleinian sense, with its connection to unconscious sadism toward women and mothers.

If an analyst works correctly, if he succeeds in hearing men and women beyond a certain point in the war of the sexes, a point of masculine defiance, of relation to castration, it is manifestly the question of the mother which arises in analysis with a male analyst, in a massive way, as the first object, the first investment, of all that a mother was for a child. The omnipotence of the mother can take a thousand and one forms. For example, women analysands may desire to stop the analysis with a man and to go to a woman. This might be good, positive for the analysis, but may be lived by the male analyst at the unconscious level in a very painful, detrimental way because not only will the analyst feel dispossessed, he will feel the need to be a good mother. He will try to hold on to a place that he cannot have. As an analyst, he will have to mourn the mother which he is not. One might say that the analyst has to mourn his lack of omnipotence. But that is an abstract formula. What the analyst teaches us is that behind each abstract formula there is a fantasy which cannot be more precise and articulate. If one says that each analyst has to mourn his lack of analytical omnipotence, one has the impression of having resolved the problem; in fact nothing has been resolved because one has not spoken about the real problem. Every male analyst has to mourn his relation to his own mother and to not being a mother, the very concrete fact of not occupying the place that he desires to occupy, and of being totally dispossessed of that place that a mother and other women can hold. It is the question of the feminine identification of the analyst and, when looked at from this perspective, his own castration.

Freud could not tolerate it. For example, he recognized having totally misunderstood female homosexuality and the place of the mother in women's psyche in "The Case of Dora." He could only imagine himself as an analyst in a place which excluded the mother as the Other. Either he had to be everything in the transference, or there was no analysis. And the idea that there could be some feminine aspect in addition which would not be taken up in the transference could not be accepted by him. His women patients had to impose that on him.

Men analysts who are capable of listening to women have resolved the problem of their relation to the mother, to femininity, of what they cannot give, of the places that they cannot hold. And they have the power not only to tolerate but also to accept that a woman in analysis might want to speak to another woman and be able to say so.

This problem also has to be faced with children. There again one is confronted with all these questions, and one might say that if one were a woman, a mother, the analysis would work differently and much better. On the level of the countertransference, it is essential to be conscious of and able to remain in one's place and especially not to want to play the mother's role, or to want to be the father if that means to exclude totally the feminine, the maternal. The analyst is always confronted with fantasies that give form to the place he has trouble holding on to.

The analytic process is permanently located in the connection of each individual to the other sex, which underlies the realm of fantasy. This brings specific problems to men which they must be conscious of in theory and also in their own analysis. I think that many male analysts who try to invent questionable physical techniques, such as massage and relaxation to solve what language does not seem capable of accomplishing, want as analysts to occupy the place of women more than they realize. They cannot tolerate their own limits or that of analysis in general because it brings them back to the question of sexual difference. At that moment they act as if their deep desire as an analyst was always to be man *and* woman, as if they could not admit that there could be an Other: other sex, other analysts, and also women analysts. They have trouble in admitting that there is an impossibility which is part of the Real. Since this impossibilty cannot be stated, they transgress it. The analysis should answer everything. It is clear that the difficulty in locating this impossibility becomes linked (and this also creates the symptom) to the extreme difficulty and resistence of recognizing and locating the Other. One cannot locate a limit or an impossibility without recognizing alterity.

A male analyst must sometimes speak of what it would be like to have an analysis with a woman. It is sometimes a resistance; the patient risks posing the same problems with a woman as a man. However, the issue is more complicated. There is a dimension of illusion and of ensnarement in the confrontation of one sex with the other. But what is important and may have value for interpretation in such cases is the recognition of the other sex for the patient and at the same time for the analyst. Every time that the analyst (and psychoanalysis in general) has a position that consists, under the pretext of transference, of wanting to occupy all places, there is something which leads to enclosure. When you ask me if one can be a feminist and a

Lacanian at the same time, if someone thinks that being a Lacanian means having an answer for everything, identifying with a discourse that is dead, fixed, beyond change, and not having any connection with the Other, one cannot be a feminist and a Lacanian, for to be a feminist means to pose the question of the other sex.

If, however, being a Lacanian means to find oneself in a discourse which acknowledges its debt toward Freud but which submits itself to the Real and does not stop being reshaped by the question of the Other, one must recognize that while remaining deeply Freudian on the question of the privilege of the phallus, Lacan has considerably displaced the question of femininity. Like Freud as well as in spite of him, a whole part of Lacan's advance follows the difficult ackowledgment of the weight of the Real, as he called it, of the difference of the sexes.

four

Patrick Guyomard: 2

What is your new book on Antigone about?

It is a fairly ambitious book, one of whose objectives was to create an afterward to Lacan and therefore to provide a reading of Lacan with Lacan. That is, to consider Lacan with Lacan the way Lacan read Freud with Freud. That does not mean considering Lacan's thirty years of text, of thought, as a continuous movement but rather, seeking from the analyst's place what the sources and the questions were that Lacan was dealing with: to single out the questions that Lacan asked himself and the answers that he found and to understand why Lacan changed his mind on whatever position. We can simply say that there were a number of crises with Lacan, intellectual and analytic in his work, in which he says contradictory and different things. I think that each time he resolved problems differently. The beginning is not more or less interesting than the end or the end more or less interesting than the beginning.

It's the same thing as with Freud. There are concepts as with Freud; there are different topics, such as the death drive, narcissism, which appear at a certain moment but were not there before. There are questions posed in *The*

Interpretation of Dreams that disappear and are never taken up again by Freud. Problems that he speaks of to Ferenczi in his correspondence he never takes up again in any of his other writings.

The point of departure of my work as a psychoanalyst working and thinking after Lacan is to consider Lacan in the same way: leaving a position of Lacanian orthodoxy and trying to find the sources, the questions, the thoughts. Therefore I consciously took up something that I considered to be a very precise change in Lacan's thought, between 1960 and 1964—which had two contradictory theses. We can characterize them in the following way: in 1960 he, in a way, idealized Antigone. He said that she represented pure desire, the pure desire for death. And consequently he thought that she represented the ultimate point of analysis, its final resolution, and therefore the ideal for the analyst. An analyst constantly refers to his own analysis, and what we expect is that the analyst is able to terminate his (her) own analysis. What does it mean to terminate an analysis? Everyone asks the same question. The figure of Antigone represents fidelity, the passing from an archaic, tyrannical temporality to a democratic political mode. This touches on questions which are theoretical, social, and political with regard to psychoanalysis today and in the future. In 1960 Lacan had a certain position. In 1964 he held the reverse position. He walked away completely from an idealization of Antigone and the ideal that she had represented for the analyst. Now Lacan says that the analyst's desire is not a pure desire. That is to say, the analyst's desire is not Antigone's. In the time between 1960 and 1964 there was an enormous number of writings: there was Lacan's text on Kant and Sade, that is, another theory of desire, another position with regard to perversion, and the relation between the masculine and the feminine, that is, sadism and the murder of the feminine. In 1964 Lacan gets away from that.

I wanted to rapidly and concisely write this book that concerns this crisis. It is a dense work because I have many things to say, and I have no doubt that I will be misunderstood and criticized. But I knew that I had to say those things.

At the same time there is in this book an interior debate around and with Lacan, in which I am implicated, and where I put myself in the scene. That is to say, a polemical and strong writing which has both pleased and displeased, and that's what I wanted. It is a work that was written not as a reaction, but from a distance when lucidity could occur. I deliberately wanted to write a text that was short, clear, dense, and trenchant, which was also a text from which I could separate myself. I wrote it continuously in one and a half months. There are points on which I don't take a position because I don't know the answer. Others I take a strong position on, perhaps rightly, perhaps wrongly. I wanted it to be that way. And I ask the psychoanalytic community to grant me the right to write on things I don't know about, to break a relation with Lacan in which all those who write are in a position of knowledge and therefore of academic exactitude. I am an academic myself and have great respect for writing in the university, but I wanted to be given the right not to know everything that I was saying.

Would you speak more about pure desire?

This is a term used by Lacan. Lacan spoke about a pure Symbolic, a pure Real, and he says that the desire of the analyst is not a pure desire. Pure means three things: first there is a Kantian reference. And that refers to something which we could call the essence of desire. Why does Lacan call it a pure desire? This poses an enormous problem. It is a charged and evocative term. What is it about desire that owes nothing to anything but itself (*ce qui du désir ne devrait rien d'autre qu'à lui-même*)? As Lacan says, it is not far from being the desire for death in its pure state: in Freudian terms, the pure death drive. However, one can see in this purity a madness because, as Freud said, human life can only exist with the intertwining of drives, and the unraveling of the drives of life and death. That is, the death drive in its pure state is pure repetition, i.e., the negative therapeutic reaction, and finally the failure of analysis. Since Lacan interprets repetition as a structure of language, the pure desire for death is a Hegelian dialectic. It is negativity. Antigone is the image, the myth of this purity, and it is for this reason that Lacan doesn't hold on to his first position because he realizes that this form of purity is deadly. To have as a model an incestuous one is a negation of any alliance, of all impurity, the impurity of history and the origin of everyone. Before becoming the children of language and of speech, we are the children of a father and a mother; we are men or women, and we belong to a given history, a given culture. And all this constitutes a fundamental impurity.

Could the myth of Antigone replace the myth of Oedipus?

It is a realization of the myth of Oedipus; it is included in the myth of Oedipus. However, on the question of the relation of men and women, masculine/feminine, my book addresses Lacanians, through the analysis of Antigone in which there is the desire of Jocasta, which is posited as murderous. There is in the issue of responsibility for life that is thrown on the backs of women a sort of misogynistic position, a hatred of the maternal. The maternal is deadly, and this is complicated for Antigone who incarnates the deadly maternal since she is the glorious mirror. Antigone is the daughter of the mother who killed herself. Antigone enacts her own suicide and the impossibility of being a mother. The curse perpetrated on the mother is found in a totally symmetrical fashion in the suicide of Creon's wife and the suicide of Jocasta. I agree with Lacan that Antigone is also suicidal. She seeks death in contrast to her sister, Ismene, who takes another path. In Sophocles there is distancing from God. In Aeschylus, the Greek city-state does not choose between the two sisters. Antigone represents a time of democracy, but at the same time, she brings with her the danger of an archaic, incestuous origin.

There is a confusion among numerous analysts who compare the figure of Antigone in my book with Christ. That signifies a misunderstanding on their part, an ignorance of Greek tragedy, and a superimposition of the sacrifical figure of Christ on that of Antigone. This is a total misinterpretation: political, historical, and also Lacanian. Because if one sees in Antigone the figure of Christ and therefore a Christ-like model for psychoanalysis, this poses many problems for the future of psychoanalysis and the images that represent the place of the analyst. One makes a total misinterpretation of the psychoanalysis of Freud, Lacan, and of Antigone which has no Christ-like or biblical reference. It comes from the fifth century B.C. The perspective on guilt, destiny, history, election, death, redemption, the Messiah in Christianity, have no reference to Antigone.

In the United States one hears a great deal about the desire of the patient. We don't speak that much about the desire of the analyst.

The analyst is not the civil servant of a science or a sect, certainly not of a religion—or even of a certain discourse. And in an even more violent way, all discourse and the findings of science are able to be perverted according to the use one makes of them. The question about the desire of the analyst is in its domain the same as that of the ethics of the researcher in the scientific field. One sees this problem in genetic engineering and in the atomic bomb, for example. There is a position in science which consists of working only for science; this can give birth to the best or the worst. At some point, the man of science can decide to stop his research because he is afraid of the results it could lead to. Therefore the desire of the scientist touches on the responsibility of science. For the psychoanalyst it is similar. Psychoanalysis is a technique that can lead to better or worse. It can become a technique of subjection, to speak of the worst: a completely subtle transmission of ideology, of the norms of a given society, or even theology, religious questions concerning the life of children, of women, of the future of couples. What determines this besides scientific acquisition is the desire of the analyst. As with parents, it's not a question of pedagogy, but a question of their desire that is most fundamental. In the field of psychoanalysis, its future, its survival in relation to the ideals of a society which might want to use psychoanalysis for repressive political ends or doctrinal purposes concerning women or religion depends on the desire of the analyst. That is to say that the analytic community defines what psychoanalysis is and therefore decides to speak or to remain silent. For example, one sees in political regimes how psychoanalysis can be allowed or prohibited, how in Latin America it is compromised by different dictatorships. There are a thousand social temptations to enlist psychoanalysis, which has an extremely powerful discourse, in the service of politics.

The question of the mental health of the child, the treatment of children, of madness—in all this what is important is the desire of the analyst. That's a way of saying that the ethics of the analyst are fundamental for everyone.

Selected Bibliography

La jouissance du tragique: Antigone, Lacan et le désir de l'analyste. Paris: Aubier, 1992.

five

François Roustang

What brought you to psychoanalysis?
I wanted to be analyzed because I wasn't feeling good, and a few years later
I changed my profession. I said to myself, "Why not become an analyst?"
It's a very complicated story.

What was your former profession?
I was a Jesuit in charge of a theological review.

Who are your patients? What proportion are men? Women?
Half and half.

Don't women want to be analyzed by women?
That's not my impression. I have men who want to see a man and women
who are ready to see a woman or a man. I have a good number of very different types of male analysands. One of the characteristics of my practice is
that I have many Jews, but also people who come from everywhere:
Algerians, Moroccans, South and North Americans. A lot of foreigners and

often Jews, probably because there are many Jews who are part of the French intelligentsia. In general, my patients have been relatively cultivated.

What do women want in analysis, and what do men want?
I hate generalizations. I think that each person who comes to see me is asking for something different. I can say that I am in a different relation with women and with men, but their initial need isn't really different. What do people want in general? They want to live better because they don't get along any more with their friends, their spouses, because they cannot work any more; some are so inhibited that they cannot even live. But this is pretty much the same for men and for women.

You say that you are in a different relation with women and with men.
Yes. What strikes me is that all that I learned as an analyst I learned from women. I think—and this is perhaps one of my preoccupations—that women are much closer to life in a very general sense of the term than are men. Here I am taking the expression from Winnicott. In women there is a continuity between the life of language and the life of instincts, whereas with men there is a much greater discontinuity. In general, it is much more difficult for men to bring to the surface their deep concerns and their connection to life, to instinct. Essentially women have taught me what I have called in a book: "*l'élémentaire du rapport à l'autre*" (the basic connection to the other), "*le jeu de l'autre*" (the interplay with the other). Women pose the radical question: Are we separate individuals? It is fundamentally that. While men have the conviction that they are separate individuals, for women this is not at all evident. This is probably because of the mother/child relationship, especially the mother/daughter relationship, something immediate which pertains to the reality of life in a way which is not perceived by men.
When Freud speaks, for example, of the mother/daughter relationship, he says that it is a totally lost continent like the Minoan-Mycenean civilization, while he himself claims to be a man of the classical age.

What I mainly learned, thanks to women in analysis, is that there are connections of an immediate order among human beings that are decisive for all relations, which at the same time are hardly perceived and are much less thought about by men. There is here a whole series of questions to pose to psychoanalysis itself, which doesn't have the theory that would allow it to understand this precisely. Psychoanalysis is constructed entirely as a system of defense in order that this immediate relation not be apparent, and so one turns away from the essential question. One uses words which are totally insufficient: *narcissism, primary narcissism, original narcissism,* because one does not have the concepts that would allow us to think directly of this immediacy. I think that a man like Winnicott perceived that very well, and he got out of this difficulty through his theory of games.

Yesterday a "borderline" patient said to me: "I don't know if you can understand, but for me humanity in the most specific sense of what a person is in relation to the totality of vegetable, animal, and mineral life is something extremely fragile." And she told me that most people think or seem to live with the idea that they are distinct individuals and that they consider human character as definitively acquired. "For me," she added, "this is uncertain." What she was saying in a very precise way is something that I feel at certain moments of analysis and that exists throughout life when one knows how to listen to what is happening. That is, the principle of all human relations is a nonrelation in which we don't know who is who. There is a kind of mixture of substances that one sees very clearly in the mother/child and especially the mother/daughter relationship.

This is something that women forced me to hear—as if they banged me on the head for me finally to acknowledge it. And afterwards I was able to discover it among men also. I was able to get men to speak of it. But it is women who live this spontaneously and maybe psychotics also. For me there is a very close relationship between psychosis and this immediate connection where individuality is not exactly asserted. In many cases the impression of the psychotic is that he is absorbed or rejected by the other. Freud could only glimpse this. For example, he says very clearly, in the text on negation, that in the beginning there was an expulsion or an appropriation. I think that this core is found in all analysis, and again it is women who are completely ready to make of that something totally pertinent. At least when they are not deformed by intellectuality.

We often hear that men analysts need to have a feminine side in order to be analysts. What does that mean and do you agree?
I would say that that is a cliché. For ten or fifteen years people have spoken about the feminine aspect of the male psychoanalyst. That bothers me. Since Freud one can no longer doubt our bisexuality; in fact, we all have feminine aspects. But if that means anything for me—although I wouldn't pose the question in these terms—it essentially means to carry within oneself, in anguish, a nonresolved problem, maybe one impossible to resolve. It's to carry something within and to let it work on itself. This is something very important for an analyst. We don't immediately hear or we don't understand what is happening in the other, but we have to ruminate on it, let it pass through, or be penetrated by it. And this is an aspect which I think is feminine, that is, a woman receives much more of an ensemble of impressions than a man does.

I would say that a crude difference between a man and a woman is that a man catalogues the parameters that he is able to understand and does not want to hear about those parameters that he cannot master or that he cannot codify or separate. A woman does not work that way at all. She allows a multitude of impressions to fill her, and that doesn't bother her at all. She doesn't have the need to cerebralize immediately, but from her impressions, she extricates something. For example, it happens very often when I go somewhere with my wife that she says: "I can't connect with that man or that woman at all." "What does that mean?" I ask. "Well it's like that." This is very important, and afterwards, I pay more attention. I sense that she perceives something that I haven't perceived, something that she's not able to explain yet. Two, three days later, but not immediately, she may say something while I have noticed nothing. I think that women are sensitive to many more elements and parameters which constitute a person or a discourse or a landscape or whatever you wish and that they don't need to master them to allow them to enter inside them.

Where does this sensitivity in women come from? Is it biological? Are they superior?
Yes, women are superior to men. Fundamentally everything is biological *and* cultural. One cannot go along with such banalities as: "It's because she

can have children that...." I know nothing about this. These are gratuitous hypotheses. I would say that we all have this global sensitivity. And after years of analysis, I distrust many more of my reflections, of my thoughts, of my ideas. And even now, when I open a book—it's even a way of working—I begin by reading through once, and afterward I sleep on it; then I reread, flipping the pages, and then I sleep and I dream, and then something new appears. In other words, it is perhaps our civilization, which codifies everything with an invasion of technology, which has made us lose this primary sensitivity. Where does that sensitivity come from? I don't know. There are biological and intellectual differences. I think that, in general, women are much closer to their bodies, to their feelings. They let themselves be more connected to their senses, while men are in a much more defensive state. One can show this in many ways: all the publications that speak about sexuality say that, in fact, sexual life for a man is something very restricted. For a woman it is something that must be in a continuum. There is preparation, a before, an after, and the sexual act is only a particular moment in the whole of life. While for a man it is only that. I don't know if this is biological, but in any case it is a commonplace to say that the sexual life of a man has nothing to compare with the sexual life of a woman.

Why, if they are superior, do women have a secondary position in politics, in religion, and so on?
It's tradition.

Yes, but there are reasons for tradition.
I think that first of all it is because of the role of men in political life for thousands of years—at least since the beginning of our civilization. There were matriarchal societies, but since the Sumerian and Roman empires it is men who have ruled politics, and therefore it is men who rule and dominate—at least apparently. But I think that women have always had their own power. There is a text of Luce Irigaray which says that in the gospels men and women are equal; but in fact there are inequalities. The twelve apostles are all men. I think that in our civilization there is a very narrow boundary between politics and religion. Furthermore, all of the great founders of religion have been men. What are the religions that were founded by women?

Not Judaism or Christianity or Islam or Hinduism. (Perhaps in the myths of South America one might find an important place given to women.) This is a historic fact that probably plays a role in giving a secondary position to women. Among the Protestants, women have access to the cult. They can preach. It is Catholicism that guards its tradition so strictly.

Do you think that there is going to be more equality?
Not at all.

So feminism is not going to have very much influence?
I know several women who are part of the feminist movement. I find what they are doing very interesting, but I wonder if very often it doesn't turn into its opposite. They protect many feminine values and show their worth but as for a profound change in our civilization, I don't think they will cause that at all.

Don't you think that there is going to be a change in the relation of the sexes?
There are changes. We can't say that the male/female relationship in the United States is the same as it is in France. I go to the United States almost every year. Women there are put in an untenable position, and this is becoming more so in our civilization. Read Bettelheim's *Surviving and Other Essays.* He says that young girls are asked to be good students, even better students than the boys. If they go to the university they have to be superior to the young men in order to be recognized. And they are told that by age twenty-five they should be married and have children. Obviously they must take care of their children. And eventually they must have a career. Being given this double job as well as having the desire for equality, women face an impossible task. It is much more difficult to be a woman today because of the feminist movement. It is an aberration. However, I have nothing against feminism. It is a completely valuable movement in our civilization. That women can work, that they can be equal is excellent, for they are as capable as men in all fields. When I was young, people said that girls should finish their education with primary school. Then it was secondary school. And we saw that the girls succeeded as well if not better than boys

in secondary school. We see now that young women succeed very well in the university. One even sees that in certain competitive exams where there used to be a separation of men and women, which was eliminated for reasons of equality, women are now taking almost all the prizes.

What should be done?
That's not my concern. I have a daughter, and I often say to her that it is a hundred times more difficult to be a woman than a man in our society. "So it's necessary that you play all your cards." She answers me. "Don't worry. You will see. I will make it."

What about the new father? Does he exist?
Certainly. In France and in the United States. But I know that my father was very involved with his children. He used to bathe us when he was free from work. It's true that men now accept taking care of the children, doing the shopping, the cooking much more readily. That's very good. But there are still men who are incapable of taking care of a baby.

If artificial reproduction takes place in the future, will that change the relation between the sexes?
Certainly. What I fear is that women will lose their distinctive qualities that they bring to civilization and humanity. But that isn't certain. I think that some women in political life in France are wonderful. We had a secretary of health (Michelle Barzac) who was very feminine, very direct in her speaking, and sometimes treated men in politics like little boys, which they are.

Are men afraid of women? If so, exactly what do they fear?
They are afraid of being understood without knowing it. It is pure panic. If a woman understands what is taking place in a man she must not tell him so. I think that this is fundamental in the male/female relationship. While a man argues about precise points, the woman sees things in general. This is not tolerable to a man.

Are women afraid of men?
Not at all on the same level. A woman might be afraid of a man who is vio-

lent, but a man is afraid of being understood, of being manipulated. Women know very well which strings to pull to make a man move.

The masculine sex has been valorized. The feminine sex is not. Are this valorization and this nonvalorization necessary for there to be a union of the sexes?
If there were a statue of a vulva on the Place de la Concorde or in Washington, I don't know if many women would tolerate it. This may be a difference with regard to visibility. Perhaps men need a visible erection of the penis in civilization whereas women need something relatively secret.

But breasts are not secret, nor is pregnancy.
The reflex of men facing a pregnant woman is like a caricature. Some are very attentive as if protecting a dangerous power. They are polite, affable. Others are angry. In the psychiatric hospitals when an intern is pregnant, one sees a deluge of politeness *and* nastiness. At this moment there is an affirmation of power in women.

Do men envy feminine *jouissance* more than women's reproductive capacities?
It's difficult to say. In dealing with feminine *jouissance*, there is an extraordinary complexity and secrecy. Many men are afraid of feminine *jouissance*. I have seen a number of cases in which men are made impotent by the demands of women and their sexual excitement. This is something which is absolutely intolerable for many men. They have an extraordinary fear of women.

What does this fear come from?
Do you think that there are causes?

We are looking for them.
It is already an enormous task to try to describe the facts. I know nothing about where this comes from. The biggest fear, which may be the source, is the fear of absorption. What is a man in front of a woman who is having an orgasm? He is completely panicked because he feels engulfed by her sexu-

ality. Some men find their pleasure and orgasm in it. But they need to let themselves go completely and to lose themselves. When one speaks about the "little death" of the sexual act, it is something very real, in particular, if the man and the woman reach orgasm together. It's so extraordinary that they both have the impression of losing themselves. I think that it is this which makes them so afraid.

Does this fear pertain to women, also?
And why would women not be afraid? Why don't some women have vaginal orgasms? There is this moment of total abandon that they cannot stand. It is a moment of loss of consciousness and also dissolution. It is this feeling of dissolution that creates fear because it represents the loss of boundaries. There is no more distancing of any kind. There is fragility, incertitude of individuation, a loss of individuation.

But don't women also desire this?
I completely agree.

Do men always make a split between the virgin and the whore?
Yes. And even women think of it, not of virgins, but of nuns and whores. But it is not a split. One moves from one to the other. The vestal becomes a prostitute. This is interesting on the level of fantasy, and it doesn't matter if the woman is a virgin or not. This is not so much a valorization of virginity. It's the fact that there is in the virgin an omnipotence which in iconography makes her inaccessible to sexual desire. And at the same time, she is able to give herself to anyone, no matter what. These are two versions of the same fantasy and it is for me a fantasy of omnipotence.

Do women also split the sexual object into the sexual guy and the good man: the good husband and good father who may not particularly attract them sexually?
I don't see women having fantasies about men who are desexualized. Sometimes women wish to have a man who doesn't think about sex any more, but I don't think that that desire has much force because when they think about their father, there is always that ambivalence between a father who is protective and who is desirable sexually.

The other part of the question is: Are women more capable of fusing these opposites: the sexual and the good, that is, the gentle, the protective, in ways that men find difficult?

I see that perfectly. Women reconcile opposites much more easily than men do.

This is important when it comes to the question of love. A woman is able to fuse experiences in a way that men cannot.

Exactly. It's interesting that a woman always looks for a man who is able to surprise her even if she is disturbed by him. If he is able to surprise her sometimes by what he does, what he thinks, this is very important for the arousal of love and desire. How many young women will say of a man, "He's a great guy. He makes me laugh." There is a connection between feminine laughter and feminine *jouissance* which is extraordinary. A young man of twenty who is able to make the girls laugh is adored because there is something explosive there. They are liberated from something through laughter.

Doesn't a man need laughter also?

He needs to make the other laugh, to show off. It's a performance. And when one sees men at a party, there is a competition as to who can produce the most laughter.

Do men speak of feminine cycles: menstruation, menopause?

I have never heard them speak about menopause. It is certainly a problem. But all this is very ambiguous. I see men who are very much afraid of women's blood, but others who are totally fascinated by it. Having sexual relations during menstruation can be something much more exciting than ordinarily. It's a kind of entrance into a woman's life, which is sexually exciting. Some civilizations wanted to separate the two. Among Jews, even currently, the woman is unclean during menstruation. And it is perhaps this impurity which fascinates and attracts sexually.

The same goes for sexual relations during pregnancy. Some men are panicked at the idea of penetrating a pregnant woman. Others, however, are excited as if in a homosexual relation, wherein the participation of a third partner becomes an extraordinary challenge. But I think that everything can be its opposite. Nothing is ever one-sided. Even if for some it is one way, for others it is different.

What about defloration, to use an old-fashioned term?
I have heard some young people say that it is an impossible act while others are furious when a young woman tells them that it is her first time. Their answer is: "If I had known, I wouldn't have done it."

This is a change from the nineteenth century and much of the twentieth.
Yes. There has been a great change.

Why? Is it because of birth control? If male domination has decreased, maybe there is more chance for changes for women in our civilization than you were perhaps indicating earlier. We wonder what women can do to help themselves, because what is the solution if you are so pessimistic and life is so hard for them?
Women can probably bear that.

Can we save Freud and his position on women?
I think that Freud was a pioneer who opened up many things. One can't ask him to have discovered everything. Our great mistake currently is to say, "Freud said that," and to stop there. One can still go on. This said, I think that Freud's position, like probably everyone else's, was very linked to his own idiosyncracies, his way of viewing the civilization in which he lived. We were speaking before about the mother/daughter relationship. He himself recognized that he didn't grasp it, but he didn't want to embark on that. The same thing goes for psychosis. And I think that the two elements are very linked. Freud stopped himself. When Freud speaks, in "Psychoanalysis Terminable and Interminable," of the parallel between penis envy and the fear of castration, that doesn't seem to me at all parallel. I have not seen many women speak of penis envy. I do not hear about it.

And the phallus? Do they have phallus envy?

As a symbol of power, perhaps. One certainly sees women who have a hard time accepting their femininity. But does that mean that they have penis envy? I wouldn't say so. However, the difficulty for women to accept their femininity is very common.

To what do you attribute this difficulty?

We live in a masculine civilization. Not only us. In China currently, where families cannot have more than one child, they kill the daughters. How can children not be affected by this? How often do parents say to their daughter that they wanted to have a son. And they make her feel this. I had in analysis the daughter of a wealthy man who wanted his first child to go on with the business. He managed to make of her someone totally alienated. Because the father and the mother also (how many times does one hear this?) wanted to have a son, it becomes a considerable problem for the daughter to accept who she is. Does she desire a penis? It is not expressed that way. It is much more the desire to have an important position, to succeed socially, to have a name. That belongs directly to the social realm but not to penis envy. It's the weight of the social and cultural order. In families, mothers as well as fathers want to have a son. And this influences the difficulty that women have in accepting their femininity.

What is femininity? Is it the acceptance of gender?

One can define it superficially by certain behaviors. For example, a little girl will be more interested than a boy in her dress, her looks. She wouldn't tolerate having pimples, is careful about her body, her appearance. It starts there. Afterward it is a kind of relation to others, which is not a direct domination, a mastering, but is much more a game, a possibility of entering into relationships in a much more complex way.

Is this a conservative definition?

I am very conservative. According to you, what would be a revolutionary position?

Women analysts, especially in the United States, think that we could change, even abolish sexual difference. They sometimes see sexual difference as something superimposed on the more basic difference between self and other.

Would that be the negation of difference? Then one wouldn't speak any more about sexual difference and femininity.

There is a linguistic problem here. In English, the words *feminine* and *female* are often translated by the same word in French: *feminin(e)*. *Female* refers to anatomical difference alone and *feminine,* as we use it in the States, refers to socially constructed difference: interest in clothing, in beauty, which the feminist analysts in the United States would say is completely cultural. They want to get rid of it.

What would the consequences be? There are thirty-five-year-old women who are professors in the university who say, "I cannot have children because my career would be ruined. I cannot have a husband." Or they had one, but after a while they had to give him up since they were five hundred miles away. And the men—no problem: no wife, no children, no problem. When they are forty they get married, have children. What can women do? They are unhappy. When they are twenty there are no problems, but at thirty-five it is different. Therefore does femininity not exist?

What's the solution?

I don't have any. In France it is easier, since France is smaller than the United States. One can travel one hundred and thirty miles away to teach. In the United States, distance is more of a problem. And there, a woman is even told not to have any children when she is writing her thesis. This is terrible! I would say that the success of American feminism is good, but it has its consequences. And it is the men who win because for them there are no problems.

Selected Bibliography

Dire Mastery: Discipleship from Freud to Lacan (Un destin si funeste, 1976). Baltimore: Johns Hopkins University Press, 1982.

Psychoanalysis Never Lets Go (Elle ne le lâche plus, 1980). Baltimore: Johns Hopkins University Press, 1983.

The Quadrille of Gender: Casanova's Memoirs (Le bal masqué de Giacomo Casanova, 1984). Stanford, CA: Stanford University Press, 1990.

The Lacanian Delusion (Lacan de l'équivoque à l'impasse, 1986). New York: Oxford University Press, 1990.

─────────── six

Serge Lebovici

Has adolescence always existed? Has the sexual revolution changed the concept of adolescence?

This is a sociocultural question. You know that there are many works that consider adolescence in theory as a time of passage, but it is not very well defined on the psychological level. It is true that during the preceding centuries, in any case before the French Revolution, children entered into adult life very early. The biological evolution wasn't taken into account. Actually there are two sorts of societies. In nonindustrial societies adolescence is only a period of passage, even though it is marked by rites of transition between the status of the child and that of the adult, rites which are always marked by initiation and pain. In industrial societies adolescence takes on more and more importance; however, it is linked to puberty, which is a chronological evolution that is not well defined. The appearance of secondary sexual characteristics, menstruation, breasts, facial hair are its signs for the public. But that said, it is a period that tends to stretch out, to appear earlier because nourishment in industrial societies brings about earlier manifestations of puberty. Above all, adolescence extends itself in the other direction, because entrance into industrial society comes much later; the needs of adolescents in our society, their dependence, increases because of the fact that they cannot earn a living. The length of studies and the technologization of the professions have increased. Adolescence is a period that tends to have a lot of importance because it is a social class that has money and at the same time doesn't, and has needs that it satisfies, particularly in the sexual sphere. Therefore the process of becoming an adult, insofar as it is extended, is made more difficult.

We wrote a book, which appeared a few years ago, called *Adolescence terminée, adolescence interminable* (Terminable and Interminable Adolescence). What we wanted to show in this book—and there is a second, *Devenir adulte* (Becoming an Adult), which deals with this question—is that the process of becoming an adult is a new and difficult process, and there is, as Freud said, a biological base in men and women which prevents them from completely achieving their destiny. Becoming an adult or maturization or *maturescence* is a process which hits up against a wall, which is not only social but also psychological and biological. There is also this new phenomenon of interminable adolescence. It is not simply a sociological process. It is a process which brings limits and difficulties. Adolescence now extends through all of life because the parents want to remain adolescents to imitate their children. They envy them because of their sexual freedom that they didn't have. Therefore the middle-aged adults who stroll in curious outfits on Sundays in New York as well as in Paris are the people who are always in the process of becoming adults, even when they are parents or grandparents. Adolescence is a new model.

Does interminable adolescence exist more among men than women?

It is more marked among men. Thirty, forty years ago, a great many young men were workers. After a very limited apprenticeship, after their military service, they got married. Now they don't want to marry. They want multiple experiences of living together, and they meet young women who also have a professional life, who don't want to have children too early. Therefore the social reason for men to start a family and be responsible for it, to be the head of a family, no longer holds. This sociocultural modification coincides with the young men's desire to remain adolescent and the impossibility they face in doing anything else. Therefore the situation is more difficult for them than for the young women. And the transformation of the role of young women in society is more favorable than for men. The men are balancing on the edge in a precarious equilibrium more than women are. But women are also in a precarious position because their traditional role is now put into question. In France, men used to be drafted when they were in their early twenties even when there was no war. They had a fiancée. They got married and made a living. Men knew what they were going to do. Now it's not like that at all.

The change for women has been for the young ones, not the older ones, who are not doing too well at this moment. Young women find work and adjust very well to their independence, in relation to their parents, who accept their emotional and sexual independence. It is much easier for the young women than for the men.

With regard to female puberty, the psychoanalytic literature speaks very little about menstruation. Male analysts don't mention breasts, etc.

Neither do women. The nourishing breast is mentioned but not the erotic breast. You don't find anything in the psychoanalytic literature about the erotic breast. I am not the only one to say this. I don't know why. It merits a reflection that I cannot do like this. But it is evident that the literature concerning the breast is about the breast as a metaphor for orality. There is the good breast, the bad breast, but it is not the woman's breast. It is a metaphorical breast, the partial object of the infant.

There are some analysts who speak about nursing. The psychiatrists and psychoanalysts who deal with infants have to take into account the reality of the woman's breast, but not the erotic breast. In fact, the infant and the mother have an erotic relationship with the breast.

But we were speaking about adolescence. The first menstruation has not been extensively studied in the psychoanalytic literature, but adolescence in the psychoanalytic literature is also very limited. What I told you before about adolescence is not at all psychoanalytic; it is sociocultural. The reconstruction of adolescence is a subject which has never been well treated, to my knowledge. I could speak to you about my adolescence very openly. In analysis people have a lot to say about their adolescence. But a reconstruction of adolescence, in the sense that one reconstructs the infancy of an analysand, is done very rarely, and I think that this is a lack in the majority of analysts. I have a lot of patients for whom I think that the reconstruction of their adolescence is essential. I have a patient at this moment with whom I have a lot of problems, a very pretty and intelligent young woman who hides herself in a terribly unhappy life, although socially she plays an interesting role. She had a very weird adolescence where she stayed at home in her room, pretending to be sick. Doubtless she had a serious depression. She lived with her mother and father during this period of adolescence, a father somewhat diminished by the mother. All this is difficult to reconstruct and does not occur in the literature.

In France we have some interesting studies on adolescence, but they are still very fragmented. There is much to be done. There is a pathology of adolescence that psychoanalysts are interested in, in the United States as well as in France, which concerns eating disorders; anorexia and bulimia have reached massive proportions. It is an epidemic.

Is it more important now than previously?
More important, more serious because when I began to practice psychiatry, anorexia was exceptional, and you could cure it easily. The patient was put in the hospital for three or four months, separated from her family; she ate, she gained weight, and it was over. But now these are illnesses that can last all one's life. And you know well that, in the United States and France too, bulimia wrecks havoc. We have now formed a network of scientific research on bulimia which is sponsored by the National Institute of Mental Health, an institute which has many laboratories working on bulimia, which is now a plague. There is a true bulimia among young girls who want to get skinny, who make themselves vomit, who take laxatives, but who run to the refrigerator to eat butter, who munch all day long, and complain about being too fat. This is truly a new problem of adolescence.

Is this a problem that is more common among young women than young men?

Yes. Above all, young women. There are boys who are bulimic also. There are also obese young boys who eat a great deal, but there is a great difference between obesity and bulimia. Obesity is eating too much. Bulimia involves the need to eat too much and to suffer. It's having a compulsion to eat. True bulimia is a frightful illness. There are many who suffer from it, in part because there is a cultural pressure not to have a full figure, large breasts, etc. This is a new pathology.

How do you account for it?

First, because civilization is such that we have a lot to eat. In Africa there is no bulimia. Second, because the traditional female figure with big breasts and somewhat large buttocks is prohibited by high fashion. The designers are homosexuals who don't like women with feminine figures. They like androgynous women. Therefore they have massively imposed their ideas. Along with that, the women's revolution has caused women to want not to be different from men. Therefore we have unisex styles, which have created a state of mind in which one must not have curves; it's necessary to be thin, svelte, muscular, and athletic. It is on these grounds that bulimia has taken a dramatic form. I'm not saying that there were never people who wanted to be thin, but now it has become an illness of civilization in which psychoanalysis has something to say.

What are the psychoanalytic reasons for this phenomenon?

I don't think that psychoanalysis can explain it. It belongs to the sociocultural order. I think that psychoanalysis can study individual responses to a phenomenon. Having to be thin and to fast is a sociocultural phenomenon of advanced industrial civilization. The way each one is going to respond—there, perhaps, psychoanalysis can say something. I can speak of the cases that I have.

Is anorexia the wish to die?

No, on the contrary I think that it means to want to live. An anorexic is a hyperactive person. She does a lot of things, is an excellent student. She doesn't sleep. There is an excellent formulation in a book by Evelyne and Jean Kestemberg, which is about the woman and the body. She says something about its symbolism: anorexia is the orgasm of hunger. It's the orgasm of the void. The *jouissance* of the anorexic is to feel herself empty. She doesn't feel hunger any more. All becomes the *jouissance* of the body. There is a destruction of the body, but there is no idea of suicide that controls her. There is the idea of being stronger than anybody else and of living with a body that is empty and clean.

At the beginning there is a rejection of the feminine sexual form and often menstruation decreases, but the dominating phenomenon is the idea of emptiness.

Doesn't this emptiness deny female sexuality?
Certainly. It begins with a fear of sexuality, and then it becomes a new form of sexuality. You know, some bulimics are also anorexic. There are anorexics who arrive through bulimia, who eat enormous amounts which cause them to vomit. This is another form of anorexia, which always takes place through the feeling of what is happening inside the body.

Is there a relation to the mother which is different today and which produces anorexia?
The relation of the adolescent to the mother is relatively different, but I don't think that one is able to link this to anorexia. I don't think that anorexia occurs because of the new relation to the mother. It is true that adolescent girls are much more independent of their mothers; it is also true that there is a sexual life that the mother tolerates or favors or doesn't tolerate, but now we are in the cultural sphere. We are not dealing here with fundamental changes because when adolescents have children they remain like their mothers, dependent on the baby's grandmothers. And the grandmother becomes an essential person. All that persists in actual society. One of my friends and colleagues speaks of the debt of life. The young woman, the young mother always owes the life that she gives to her child to her own mother. I am speaking of "fantasmatic interruptions" and I think that all babies are the children of the grandparents more than the parents.

Is the mourning for the first object of love in the Oedipal stage more difficult and complicated for the girl than for the boy?

That's for sure. What you say is in the Freudian tradition. But finally the mourning for the object of love is not a Freudian term. It's a recent term introduced by Michel Fain, who says that one must mourn the Oedipal object. I don't think that one ever finishes mourning the loss of the Oedipal object. It is an interminable mourning, and it is much more difficult for the girl in the Freudian tradition. There are two more-or-less equal love objects for the girl. She begins with the mother; then she has to change to the father, but the mother remains a predominating object of love, even if she is hated. Love and hate go together. If there is mourning, it is more difficult for a woman than a man because she has two superegos: father and mother remain for her in a much greater state of indeterminacy than for the boy. The ambiguities are much greater for her.

Do you agree with Freud when he says that women are more narcisssistic than men and that their superego is weaker?
When you pose the question like that, it is always difficult to answer yes or no. It's clear that when one speaks of the relation of the objects, a narcissistic relationship with the object is more feminine than masculine. The man is more dependent in terms of the relation to the object. But in terms of the displaying of narcissism, I believe that it is absurd to say that the woman does so more than the man. The difficulties of narcissistic investment and narcissistic fragility are probably even more important among men, who who are more fragile biologically, who die earlier, who can realize their accomplishments less, especially if they don't belong to a social or intellectual sphere where they can make things happen. The working man doesn't have a narcissism that is very gratified by his life while a woman who has children is constantly reinforced narcissistically because she sees what she has produced.

There are certain things in relation to women that you don't want me to say, but just the same I think that there is a new aspect to the psychoanalysis of women, in which men analysts play a part in dealing with infants. This interaction is a completely new problem. Let us say that, for the last several years, analysts in France and the United States, although not in England, have been playing an important role in the treatment of babies. The women now appear as mothers, holding their babies in their arms. There has been a lot of work which has modified many perspectives on the woman and on the infant. And on the effect of the infant on the mother because it is the baby that acts so much on the mother. He depends on her surely and on others, but the mother depends on the baby for her femininization, her maternalization. It's the baby who causes this and has a considerable power over the woman. This is a very important analytic subject.

We have a whole network of research on it, and we aren't the only ones. This is very developed in the United States also. It is a new analytic domain.

Would you speak about the reverie of the mother?
I think that what separates me from Bion when he speaks of the mother's capacity for reverie is this: he says that the baby goes through mortal anxieties and that he projects these onto the mother. The mother must be capable of "metabolizing" them, of fantasizing them and of acting in such a way that the baby can structure itself from this maternal reverie. I think that that is a totally theoretical conception. What happens is that a baby and its mother are two beings who interact with each other on the plane of behavior. That's been well known since John Bowlby valorized the theory of attachment, which is accepted by everyone. But it is much more important if one considers what happens between the baby and the mother on the affective and fantasmatic plane. For me, and not only for me, between them what is visible at every moment and what is remarkable is an affective harmony, an affective accord. That is, for example, when the mother says "ah," and the baby moves its legs at the same time. Psychophysiologists have studied this capacity for synchronization of the baby and the mother, who feel the same thing, who share the same affect. I call this an emotional bath. And it is in this emotional bath that the first representations of the baby are created, according to a mechanism that psychoanalysts know well: the representation of affect. The first representation of the mother that Freud described in the framework of primary identification is organized in affective interactions.

On the other side, what I call fantasmatic interactions, is the fact that when the mother holds a baby in her arms, her entire mental life is implicated. I am not saying, like Bion, that she is dreaming. It's true that she's dreaming. But all of her mental life is implicated as well. That is, her Oedipal experiences and also everything that was transmitted to her by successive generations, by the baby's grandparents, by people who are dead, the people that one respected and those that one feared, all that we can call inter-generational transmission. That's what I think is happening at that moment.

And the new father?

The fathers contribute to the care of raising the children. They are partners in the upbringing, which they were not thirty or forty years ago. But the movement of the new father is one of both equality and sexual ambiguity. It is not true that the new father acts like the mother when he takes care of the baby. He has a different way of doing it that we have studied a lot. For example, the father who holds a baby in his arms holds it higher than the mother. The mother holds the baby against her chest. This is programmed genetically. The mother has secretions from the axillary glands and the rising of the milk when she feeds the baby. Since the mother's breast is an erogenous zone, she has pleasure when she holds the baby the way that she does. And the father has pleasure holding the baby against his neck because the neck is erogenous for men. Furthermore, mothers rock horizontally; fathers rock vertically. What I want to say is that the father is a good partner in raising the children, but he doesn't have the same way of doing it as the mother. The reaction of anxiety that we call the fear of strangers does not apply to the father. It's true that the father is not a real stranger although he is a stranger metaphorically. One could say that the Oedipal stage is a metaphor for the introduction of the father into the representation of the baby. Although the father is in the life of the baby much sooner now, he is recognized very differently from the mother. But there are many babies who say "Mama" to their father. That means that they wish the father were like the mother. That the father is called Mama indicates at the same time both a change of customs and also things which probably always existed but which developed further in industrial society and to which the fathers decided to react differently in a favorable fashion. These men aren't new fathers. They are fathers who are partners in raising the children.

How do you feel about artificial reproduction?

I am against the development of medically assisted procreation at inordinate cost. I can tell you a story about the first baby who was born in the faculty of medicine where I work, where we do research on early interactions between babies born through medically assisted reproduction. It is difficult to talk about because the parents don't want to cooperate. They want to erase this. I understand. They are right. When the baby was sixteen months old, I was very worried—not because he wasn't fine. He was very fine. His mother nursed him and I have a video of this. She was a very good mother. She knew what to do very well, but the father was quasi-delirious because, for him, having a baby born under extraordinary circumstances was a phenomenon that was going to single him out. It was at the moment of the Barbie trial in France, and he was saying that the child would be the new Jew. He would wear the yellow star of the children born in this new way. He made me worry.

I say that because of the media. They speak too much about it. The father was an intelligent man with a complicated history. He was a political activist who broke with his own father, who was an alcoholic. He didn't go to his father's funeral. But grandparents always play an enormous role. In fact, it was the grandparent who made him unable to be a father, for he didn't want to be a father like his father. But he became a good father. At one time when I was discussing with him his position as a father in relation to the grandfather, the baby said, "Papa." He didn't say, "Mama." That is, the baby understood very well what we were talking about. The father was an abnormal father at the beginning, and I feared many things for the baby. But when the son, at sixteen months, said "Papa," this was the decisive moment when he made a father of his father.

But medically assisted reproduction, though sometimes necessary, poses complex problems which will be felt very forcibly by the child. I do not think that it should be an alternative; procreation should remain a natural process. Coitus and reproduction should remain linked to create healthy human beings. If one separates these, we will have a dangerous, deadly utopia. I don't believe at all in the future of a humanity which will be stamped by this technology, which should be applied only when necessary.

And the surrogate mother?
I am for it. But I am against the legislation for it. One doesn't need the law. However, one has to recognize that there are dangers for the mother of

attaching herself to the baby and for the baby to have known something. In the United States, in the case of Baby M—I wrote an article on it—the final result of giving the baby to people because they have wall-to-wall carpeting at home I find enraging. They could have had a baby through other means, for example, adoption, which is a time-honored practice. In the past, if a mother died giving birth, the baby would be given to a sister, who was forced to marry the father. But one could have more civilized forms.

There is something that you haven't asked me about, which astonishes me: the problem of transference love. It is serious. There are many psychotherapists who have sexual relations with their patients. Many people say that this is excellent, that it is the best way of curing, that it is part of psychotherapy through the body. Here is a very important problem, which is one of the aspects of the difficulty of analysis, the transference of love from the patient to the male analyst. There are also homosexual transferences, but they are exceptional. There are also not many women analysts who sleep with their patients. This is a problem which shows that it is more difficult to be a male analyst than a woman analyst. I don't want to create a massive problem, but all that there is in men about the desire for conquest and for appropriation can be realized in a love transference. Therefore a male analyst has to be more conscious of the danger of transference, the danger of his maleness. I am not speaking of machismo, that is, his sexual identity as a male, but of the existence of a sexual excitement that is much more perceptible in him than in the woman analyst, of a desire to dominate, of violence. This is a difficult problem which requires a very good personal analysis of the man in order for him to have constant vigilance over himself with regard to knowing that it is not him the patient wants, but someone who is represented by him. It is a point that one should face frankly and that is a difficulty in psychoanalytic training.

Would it be a solution for women to go to women analysts instead of men?

No, I don't think so at all. I think that the word *seduction* is a dangerous word because everything that one puts on it is both very complex and too simple at the same time. For example, in France at this moment one speaks a lot about sexual abuse and incest. Certainly this is a phenomenon that exists, which is horrible, the violence of fathers against their daughters, but the accusations that are occurring now, of daughters who complain that their fathers are putting them on their knee—all this is becoming very problematic. I think that the United States is a little responsible for this. I worry a lot about the development of our civilization. I am not saying bravo to incest. It's not that. I think that it is necessary that the sexual violence of incest, incestuous rape, be very seriously condemned and prevented. Girls should be informed about this. But I don't think that we should create a society of informers. Seduction is exercised by the daughters too, and there are mothers who favor this. But that's not what I want to say. Seduction occurs at the level of the baby. It's the mother who seduces the baby. All of maternalization is a seduction. That is the real seduction. I don't have the time to develop this point of view now. It is evident that one must fight against rape, but there is another seduction that is more important for the construction of personality and which is necessary. The baby is seduced by the mother and it seduces the mother also.

Selected Bibliography

Dialogue with Sammy. A Psycho-Analytical Contribution to the Understanding of Child Psychosis (Un cas de psychose infantile, 1960). New York: International Universities Press, 1969. (With Joyce McDougall.)

Caplan, G., and S. Lebovici, eds. *Adolescence: Psychosocial Perspectives.* New York: Basic Books, 1969.

Widlocher, D., and S. Lebovici, eds. *Psychoanalysis in France (La psychanalyse en France).* New York: International Universities Press, 1980.

Esman, A., S. Feinstein, and S. Lebovici, eds. *International Annals of Adolescent Psychiatry.* Chicago: University of Chicago Press, 1988.

Authors Cited

Bion, W.R. "A Theory of Thinking." In *Second Thoughts: Selected Papers on Psychoanalysis.* Northvale, New Jersey: Jason Aronson, 1993.

Bowlby, John. *Attachment and Loss.* New York: Basic Books, 1969-1980.

Kestemberg, Evelyne, and Jean Kestemberg. *La faim et le corps: une étude psychanalytique de l'anorexie mentale.* Paris: Presses Universitaires de France, 1972.

seven

Horacio Amigorena

What brought you to psychoanalysis? Or is that too personal a question?

I don't think that one can really answer a question like that without a more inclusive and concrete questioning of the identity of the analyst. There are many factors involved. For example, I was in South America twenty-five years ago, and psychoanalysis was in a way a new discipline there, a revolutionary way of posing questions on identity, sexual identity, and the unconscious. But I don't really want to answer like this. Maybe I will answer this question later.

Would you describe your psychoanalytic training?

I began my training at the university. I studied philosophy and afterwards psychology in Buenos Aires. I began my analysis very early. I had a classical training at an international institute. Then I went to London and afterward to France. Therefore I had a very eclectic training with diverse orientations, which I think saved me and allowed me to enjoy a kind of liberty in relation to different schools. I don't belong to any psychoanalytic institute now.

Who are your patients? What is the percentage of men and women?

I have always had more women than men analysands, in South America as well as in France.

Why?

I cannot answer such a question and I would like very much to know why.

Some people feel that women are better analysts than men. What do you think?

I would like to speak as a patient in this case, for it is the only place from which I can answer you. I cannot judge if a woman can be a better analyst than a man. I don't think that it has to do with the fact of being a woman or a man. What I think is that analytic listening is marked sexually, that is, the difference between the sexes reveals itself at the level of listening also, and this is contrary to many very important analysts in the history of psychoanalysis who supported the idea that being a man or a woman wasn't important in being an analyst. On the contrary, I think that a man does not have the same analysis with a male analyst that he would have with a woman. But whether this is better or not, I don't know.

As a patient, I worked on some aspects of my history in a very different manner with women analysts and with men analysts. I should add that, without doubt, it is only with a woman analyst that a man is able to discover and elaborate on certain aspects of masculine identity, which risk remaining hidden with a male analyst.

Could you develop this point?

The fantasies of persecution that a man may have in relation to a woman, which refer to the fear of women, the figure of the archaic sorceress that men project onto women—I speak of my own experience—one must work through with intensity, with the weight of reality that only a woman analyst can supply.

Feminists like Simone de Beauvoir and others have said that for the liberation of women it is necessary to eliminate mythology because the images of the sorceress, for example, have in part

destroyed women. Can we eliminate the great fundamental myths, and would that be good for women?

I think that the problem is very complex. One cannot simply answer yes or no. What does it mean to eliminate a basic myth? On the level of culture, that would be impossible. What we can hope for, without doubt, is to illuminate where the myth is working and where it is destructive, in order to denounce it. An analyst has very little to say about that, because it's not his field. Elimination is not an analytic schema. Myth cannot be eliminated because it is myth that creates the subject. What I want to say is that, if a man's fear of a woman exists at the level of myth, the man does not have to be afraid of a woman precisely because there is a myth that will serve as a symbolic support, and the man in reality will therefore be able to love a woman. The myth will always be there to sustain something symbolically, something which is not going to hinder the man's real life.

The problem is not so much the myth, but rather when the myth becomes a fantasy: when a man approaches a woman and sees a sorceress. He confuses myth with reality and thinks that any woman can mask a sorceress.

Why does the man see a sorceress? Where does that come from?

I can say that for a man a woman represents the association of giving life and the power to take it away. In men's unconscious, there is an original fantasy on which his sexuality is based. If these fantasies can operate as a mythic core which won't contaminate his reality or as something that will function in his Imaginary without going outside the boundaries, that would be all right. If they could be eliminated without difficulty, it would be better, but I am very skeptical about that. I think that there were moments in history when these fantasies were eliminated, but they came back in a very brutal way. Finally, to give a clear example, when the sorceresses function at the level of fairy tales for children, that is fine. What is a problem is when the child thinks that the sorceress exists not only in myth. But if we eliminated this figure from our culture, from our Imaginary, then we would have very great danger. I think that there is a very important and also a good place for the sorceress.

There are certain feminists who think that they can eliminate elements that they don't like from the unconscious and replace them with something better.

Often it is the contrary. If one eliminates the sorceress, she may reappear in another way which would be worse for women.

Freud wrote about the split between the Madonna and the whore. Does this split still exist in men's fantasies?
I don't think that it exists on that level. We see in art history the Madonna and Venus, who represent the mother and the whore. These are subjects which are almost complementary, two fantasies which allow the man to hold on to a woman. But that doesn't mean that he has to have two women: a mother and a whore. I think that is a perversion in the domain of fantasy which ought to remain separate. On one side there is the Madonna-woman who gives life; there is also another woman on the side of seduction, with its dangers. Both of them are necessary for a man to desire. But it's not because they are necessary on the level of fantasy that the man in reality is going to identify a woman with one aspect or the other.

When this situation appears and there is a split, it is because he is in a neurosis, a perversion, or a psychosis. If he's not too perverse or neurotic or crazy, he won't make this split, and when he loves a woman he is going to desire this woman as a whore, he's going to want her to have a child for him like a Madonna, and the two sides are able to exist together in the same woman.

Do you think that women also make a split?
No. What's a Madonna? She's not a mother. It's more than that. And a whore is much more than a woman who is obliged to use her body to make a living. When I speak about one or the other, I speak of two figures that have an anchoring in fantasy, mythology in men's unconscious. There are not the same figures for the man—you won't find in any iconography the image of the father holding a child in his arms and showing it to the viewer. As for a male prostitute, it's more complicated.

Of course, there is not the same split for men as for women. But is there something comparable? For example, a woman might desire one man for his sexuality and another man to be the father of her children. That is, one man can serve a woman to satisfy her sexuality and another man to give her children and to live with her. But it isn't a split.

For men, where does this split of women into such opposing figures as the Madonna and whore come from? It's a split for women as well as men because this cleavage also occurs in their Imaginary, in their fantasies. But perhaps you don't think so.
For women these fantasies are not total.

You have written on the subject of love and death. Does the connection between them exist for women as well as men? What about love in literature? Is love different for the two sexes? Is pleasure different?
I don't like to speak of difference in a vacuum. I am afraid to speak of a woman and a man who don't exist anywhere. The question could be reformulated: How does an analyst perceive this difference? If one thinks of the pleasure that there might be in free association, in having the freedom of words in the analytic process, could the question be asked: Is there something there which is different for a woman and a man? As for sexual pleasure, I don't think that that is a serious question for an analyst. A sexologist would have something to say; I don't think an analyst would. It is hard to find a lover who is on the side of women in literature. Take Don Juan for example. That mythical figure, I think, corresponds to a very ironic fantasy in men, which is constitutive of their sexuality, a sexuality where there is only pleasure, but where at the end one finds death. Not too long ago, a woman psychoanalyst said there was one Don Juan and that afterward there were his copies. That is to misunderstand that there is a fantasy, a myth. One cannot say that there was Oedipus and after that copies of Oedipus. A myth does not exist on this level. To answer your question, there is no woman Don Juan.

There is the whore.
One has nothing to do with the other. She's not Don Juan. What you are saying is interesting and it's a good joke. I say that it's not the same because the whore and the sorceress are identities of women constructed by men. A woman doesn't choose to be a whore the same way that she doesn't choose to play the role of a sorceress. It is men who, because of a question of power, need to construct a sorceress and a whore. And I don't think that Don Juan was constructed by women. It would be playing on feminine masochism to think that Don Juan corresponds to a feminine fantasy.

Did women create myths also?

I don't know. I am not an anthropologist. But there is something in your question which makes me think and that touches on my work as a psychoanalyst dealing with women. It is the position that a male psychoanalyst takes in his analytic work. On the side of myth—I don't know how to say this—the myth of origin, there is where the analyst is identified with the mother who gives birth. It is not easy for a man to assume this identification at a certain moment in the analysis, to take the position of the fruitful mother, the mother who gives life, especially with psychotic women. As an analyst or as a supervisor of a young analyst, there is a sort of confusion, and in the countertransference fantasies, the male analyst as a fruitful mother is rather in the place of a father who gives life the way Adam gave a part of his body. In the countertransference, there is resistance to this identification, which is so problematic and necessary for the man, who clings to his feminine side knowing at the same time that as a woman he is sterile and cannot give life. These are things which are very interesting in the analytic process.

I could speak more about the construct of the prostitute and the sorceress. I don't want to make generalizations, but a man analyst may construct the whore and the sorceress in the power that he has of the cure. Yet this cannot be said so quickly.

Can this fantasy be deconstructed, and how? Could that happen in the analytic session?

In any analysis, whether with a woman or with a man, the analyst has great power.

Like the mother?

Like the mother, and also like the father, sometimes both together. In any case, to do his work the analyst is supposed to have this power without using it. This is not always the case. We all know that. When Freud wrote about transference love and the seduction of hysterics, he didn't see seduction as a defense when facing the power of the analyst. How can a woman protect herself from the master? Only through seduction. There is no other way. So the woman's seduction is a manipulation for power. It is a maneuver for protection. But what does it mean for a woman when she goes to a male analyst, a woman who may not have been listened to in her life, a woman who lived in great solitude and who all of a sudden discovers a man who listens to her fears, her desires, and fantasies? How is she not going to be seduced even if the analyst doesn't want to seduce her? Never will you find this subject treated in the psychoanalytic literature.

Maybe this subject should be spoken about more. What is the structure of the analytic work which belongs to the structure of analysis itself? There are analysts who are going to be silent about this. There are other conscious ones who recognize the kind of power that they have and who will try not to exert it; they will limit and denounce it. There are different powers that are at play, which are not the same when dealing with women and men.

As for your question about construction or deconstruction—how is it done? It's rare now, but if you take the example of the woman crushed by the fear of being a whore who takes refuge in the identification with the Madonna or vice versa, it is in linking these two figures on the level of fantasy and of myth that she permits herself to have a sexuality.

On the same subject, what role do the fantasies that an analyst has of a woman play? How does his personal life reveal itself? All these things are very important. On transference love, there is a very important bibliography in the psychoanalytic literature, but you will find very little on counter-transference love. There is almost no analytic work on it. Ferenczi used to ask that analysts speak of their own experiences. They are doing it less and less. How does an analyst live transference love? I must tell you that it has happened several times in my work, and I have been working for about twenty-five years with women who have come to see me, telling me, "Listen, I had analysis with so and so (nearly always a man) for twenty years, thirty years, and now that it is finished, I have nothing. I work but I am all alone." There had never been an acting out, and these analysts were within the norm. However, these women were leaving a very great love relationship with their analyst who, at a given moment, told them: "Madame, now it is over," and these women found themselves all alone.

What should such a woman do?

I have no answer. It's important that analysts work differently with concepts like transference love because love which goes on that way for thirty years seems suspect to me. There is really something here which doesn't work on the side of psychoanalysis. It's necessary to say that I have never seen the opposite: a man who stays with a woman analyst for twenty years.

But a woman could stay with a woman analyst?
Maybe. I won't say no. But that has never happened to me in my experience. It was always the women who stayed in analysis with the man.

Is the new romantic love between the analyst and his patient?
It may be romantic, but it's not really different from the destiny of the romantic heroines because when you see that this kind of love is paid for with a life of solitude, a life dedicated to the analysis, then I would say no and again no.

Is it like courtly love in the literature of the Middle Ages, a love which is far away, which is impossible.
Yes, but there is a love to which we can hold on for a whole life, and it is precisely this impossibility, which is furthermore always nurtured, because there is listening, and the more one is listened to the more one wants to speak. This never ends.

What do you suggest?
What I could suggest is the importance of always working with concepts like limit, with the fact that analysis is not the whole life. We should bring back the analytic work to what it was in its origins: a therapy to try to cure something. But analysis has become more and more a way of life, of love. The women I have in mind in the end have nothing.

We have recently heard that many women only want a woman analyst and not a man. But that does not seem to have been your experience.
No. On the contrary. I have had many women patients who thought that it was terrible to have an analysis with a man, but they have changed their minds. I think that that corresponds to a certain moment in the feminist movement, for which I have great respect, where women had a real need to find themselves as women excluding men. It is a moment in the personal life of the young girl or woman that is completely necessary. There

are moments in history when women have to distance themselves from men.

Do you consider feminism positive for women? For men?
For men, I think that it has been very important. I have learned a lot from feminist women writers. I have profited a great deal in exchanges with women analysts.

The English psychoanalyst Enid Balint, whom we interviewed for *Women Analyze Women*, has said that feminism is a great danger for men and because of that a danger for women too, because if men aren't happy, then women aren't happy either.
What you are saying is important. I think that there was a normative way in which a woman had to make a man happy and vice versa. And since its origins, psychoanalysis has been trapped in the way that it had to be done, in very traditional figures, that is, the couple, the relation whereby the woman becomes a Madonna for the man. But feminism—I am not now considering it as a concrete movement but rather as an ideology and in all its breadth—has grasped new ways of being happy, with a freedom which didn't exist before, and women have seized the freedom to be more of a subject than before, without being determined by men's desire. Men can be happy like never before because they are becoming free. Therefore I would say just the opposite of Dr. Balint.

Does the woman now have the freedom not to be a sorceress, even in men's fantasies?
I think that now women have the freedom not to identify themselves with these fantasies and to denounce them and to teach a man to be able to love without making a woman into a sorceress. I think that women can teach the younger generation, especially men, to be less fearful by helping them to become conscious of these fantasies, which is very important.

Is it possible that because feminism gives more power to women, it will give men another reason to fear women?
I don't think so because the power that comes from feminism, in which there are the dangers of power as in any other movement, is a power from which

men can easily protect and defend themselves. What does it mean for a woman to become a feminist? There are different types. It is the power of the subject, the power of not allowing oneself to be determined by man's desire, and I don't think that that creates fear or prevents someone from loving. For example, I think that one of the most important aspects was the changing of the customs of the fathers. Thanks to feminism, women now allow fathers to have a relation with their infants that they didn't have formerly.

What do men, patients, think of feminine cycles: menstruation, pregnancy, lactation, menopause?

It is an important question. Maybe one of the most secret aspects of feminism resides here. In a traditional way, the difference between the sexes was defined in a social sense by men as the fact of having or not having the penis. More and more men realize that the difference is in the whole body, that the body of a woman is a body in which the connection to life is totally different from the body of a man. That is something which places us at the beginning of very important changes. Furthermore, it is one of the things which is able to help men to be happier with a woman, to desire, to be able to love a body which is so much identified with life cycles, transformation, connection to time, and which is completely different from men's.

Do you think that the concept of penis envy is a projection by men, or do you think that it truly exists?

I think that it really exists. What happened is that men endlessly interested themselves in the concept of penis envy and developed it theoretically, but there was no work on pregnancy envy. This is perhaps a lack which has as much importance for men as the lack of a penis has for women. Penis envy does not exist as an important complex for women. It exists but has been exploited to identify women with lack. How does this fantasy start? What does this lack mean for the Imaginary? It doesn't mean that women want to have a penis; it is not that.

You call yourself eclectic, but who had the greatest importance in your thought? Do you think that Lacan had a good influence for women?

In my psychoanalytic training, I think that Proust counted as much as

Freud. Lacan is as important as Mallarmé. As for women, the question should be directed to them.

What are the most important questions in psychoanalysis for women today? What are the problems that women have that psychoanalysis ought to address?

There is a question which seems very important to me and which was perhaps not very explicit before: How to love a man without being trapped, without being subjected? This is a new question, historically, which was not formulated before. Maybe it was already a question for the hysteric. In any case, I believe that it is a very important question for the future of psychoanalysis. Today this question is beginning to be formulated openly. Before it didn't exist.

Some think that love is not necessary in life, especially some contemporary women.

A woman can live without a man, but it would be difficult to live without men. To love does not necessarily mean to love a man. I think that these are different questions, and this difference is very important in the analytic work.

—— eight

René Major

**We would like to know what brought you to psychoanalysis and
what your training was.**
First I studied the classical curriculum, then medicine and psychiatry, and
following that, psychoanalysis. My direction was simple and linear. There
are many analysts who go through a different route and not necessarily the
medical one. I began to practice very early, at the age of twenty-seven.

What oriented me toward psychoanalysis? That also occurred early in my
life; during the second or third year of my medical studies, I became less
interested in medicine *per se*. I started to read Freud and many other authors
in the psychoanalytic field as well as philosophy, and during my last years of
medical studies, I started analysis in order to become an analyst.

That was the direction, but this doesn't really give the motivations for
why I chose psychoanalysis. I mistrust any answer that I could give because
everything that I would say would not exhaust the question, far from it.
One might give professional reasons, personal reasons. One might try to
understand what happened in one's childhood or in the relationship with
one's parents or brothers and sisters. But I sense that something would

remain that is profoundly unknown in connection to practicing analysis. In the passage of time one could progressively discover many motives for why one became an analyst that would be explored during the long years of practice.

Where do you place yourself in the field of psychoanalysis in France?

In fact, I am not easy to place. Although I have a special place, I can also locate myself in connection with different directions. At the beginning, I started in an apparently simple way by going to an analytic institute where I followed the most direct path to become a member of that society, an affiliated member, a training analyst, as one says in the United States, and even the director of the Institute. I followed this path very rapidly but at the same time I was very interested in what was happening in the other schools. I belonged to the Paris Psychoanalytic Society (Société de Paris) and the Psychoanalytic Institute, its training branch. But starting in 1960, at the beginning of my training, at the same time that I was at the Institute, I was also following Lacan's teachings, in particular, his seminar at the Hôpital Ste. Anne, then at the Ecole Normale Supérieure. I was not the only one from the Institute to do that. There were Green and Stein and maybe some others, but it wasn't usual. It wasn't looked on with favor to follow Lacan's teaching when one was at the Institute, but I have always been sort of eclectic, and even later I attended some colloquia of the French Psychoanalytic Society (Société Française de Psychanalyse), where I participated in events with Perrier and Zaltzman, Aulagnier and Valabrega.

After having given up the directorship of the Institute in 1974, with a colleague I founded *Confrontation,* which had a certain importance in the history of psychoanalysis. There is still a review which has that title. *Confrontation,* at the beginning, was a seminar with irregular meetings where someone from another group was invited to discuss his work. Today all that seems ordinary, but that was not the case at that time. It created great turmoil. For example, that Leclaire, Granoff, and Perrier came to speak on the premises of the Institute was considered something incredible. I don't mention these three names by chance. They had been very connected at one time when they were together in the French Psychoanalytic Society.

Then there was a split, each one going to a different school. And here they met again, for the first time, to discuss ideas together.

So *Confrontation* developed by emphasizing exchanges between people from different psychoanalytic groups, but also through exchanges with those who could be considered foreign to psychoanalysis, for example, philosophers and sociologists. There were confrontations both inside and outside the psychoanalytic field.

Where do I situate myself? While still belonging nominally to the Paris Psychoanalytic Society, I hardly go there, and in fact I give presentations and lectures in different groups. I have kept myself free to move around.

Confrontation became an important movement through its regular seminars, annual conferences, debates—a whole program without giving recognized official training like other institutes. As far as I am concerned, the question of the recognition of analysts by institutes creates enormous problems. But that is another subject. In 1983, *Confrontation* was itself becoming an institution where the questions of training and recognition were more and more present. But we stopped these activities. I think that *Confrontation* fulfilled its role historically in different groups and different disciplines and not in wanting to become a new institute. In the analytic field, I consider that a certain work of questioning and creating is obliterated by institutes, where there are constraints to think in a way which conforms to an underlying ideology. For me, ideally the analytic institutes, as much as they are necessary, should be able to dismantle themselves and build themselves up again easily. This is the opposite of the institute that has a tendency to rigidify its rules.

Since its creation in 1983, I have been at the International College of Philosophy, which is not tied to a university and welcomes all disciplines. Philosophy is put first. There are also the arts, science, psychoanalysis. At the same time, what I like is that it is an institute in which nobody can make a career. For example, I am director of a program. There are about forty directors of programs, but they are only named for three years with one possible renewal. So you can see that this institute renews itself easily. That means that it is flexible. We must try to do the maximum in the minimum of time there. It's very alive and that is what I really like. I have been part of the directing committee of the International College of Philosophy, which puts me out of the scene of the official French pschoanalytic milieu, in a way. This allows me the freedom to invite people who belong to one group or another. By coming to the college, they don't feel that they are being put into a difficult position in connection with another institute.

We would like to know who your patients are. Do you have an equal number of women and men?

It's difficult to answer this question. One would need statistics. I'm speaking of twenty-five years. Now I think it's half and half.

Do you think that the questions that male analysts ask about women are the same questions that women analysts ask? Perhaps this depends on the individual analyst.

What troubles me in your question is that you ask what questions are asked by an analyst, man or woman. In principle I ask nothing, neither of a man nor a woman.

However, it might happen that I ask a question, but then it's necessary to look at the particular case. Why this or that question? Why at this moment? Would I have done it in the same way with a man? In general, it's difficult to answer this question.

Is the demand (the reason for going into the analysis) from the woman analysand different from that of the man?

Yes, but the great difficulty when one speaks about these questions is that the explicit demand can be formulated in very different ways. This leads toward something like desire, for example, which would include differences in men and women. If you ask me whether women's desire can be different from men's desire, there are varying levels of response which belong almost to the social order. Can one isolate something like feminine desire? This is a huge question that one could discuss for hours.

I wrote very little on this question, but I did write a preface entitled "*Le non lieu de la femme*" (the "no place" of the woman) for the book *Le désir et le féminin*. I don't remember if I said anything special there concerning feminine desire. Of course, there is all that Lacan said about the question that deserves thorough consideration. What Freud said first also has been diversely interpreted according to different periods and readers.

I am thinking in particular of the present, of "feminism" in quotation marks, for what is feminism? This is, again, a big question. What has been called feminism in France has had a certain favor. This means that the questions that feminism posed to psychoanalysis had a certain pertinence. There are readings of Freud and Lacan and the reading that Lacan himself made of Freud which were influenced by these questions. I don't know if this was due to the type of dialogue that there was between theoreticians of the feminist movement, some of whom were very closely connected to psychoanalysis and others who were not. Many questions were well posed and made their mark. But then I would say that, in France at present, one does not ask the questions in the same way anymore while in the United States, I think that the feminist movement continues to have the same thrust. I wonder if it is because the responses were sufficiently adequate that the movement slowed down a little, at least from what it was initially.

I am aware that I am not bringing simple answers to your questions and that it would be clearer if I could say yes or no; but for me, it is very complex because all the generalities that one can utter on the subject are always subject to caution. For example, one might say—and this belongs to the sociological order—that feminine desire in general presents itself in a more radical manner, is more anchored in ideals, more linked to the longevity of a tie; making love corresponds more to an ideal, with the least compromise possible. But it is difficult to generalize like that. It is true at certain moments, but a woman with a desire toward the other sex or the same sex may change during analysis, without one being able to predict that change.

Finally, what seems to be most pertinent is at the same time to consider elements in connection with bisexuality. That means from the masculine and the feminine of the man and the masculine and the feminine of the woman. Then one enters into the complex problems of sexuation from the psychological point of view, and I do not know if one can make a difference then between masculine and feminine desire since one must abstract from this the foundation of psychoanalysis in psychic bisexuality.

What about *jouissance*? Is there a difference between masculine and feminine *jouissance*?

I believe so, and one should try to see on which level the difference is. And here again I speak more on the clinical point and not the theoretical one. One should not forget that feminine *jouissance* may consist of something which seems—it cannot be said in another way—to be more than masculine *jouissance*. This *more* should be explained. It is more because it is not related to the sexual organ but to the phallic function in general, which means *jouissance* can be much more diffuse, can take the psychic elements which are part of the love relationship more into consideration. One might think that feminine *jouissance* could take the Other more into consideration in his alterity in the sexual difference, or in his alterity without taking into account the sexual difference. The Other could be of the same or of a different sex, but considered as other in the relationship. Some think that feminine *jouissance* reaches beyond the *jouissance* that the masculine in men achieves. However, some men may have a rapport of the same type that women have with *jouissance*, whether this rapport is with someone of the same or of the other sex.

How do women feel about men who have a similar *jouissance*?

I think that there are women who look for men with the same type of *jouissance*, and there are also the opposite. In each case, there are reasons which take into account personal history, including what Freud described as the relation to the loved one: either a narcissistic rapport, where the other is seen as a mirror of the self, or another type where one is more centered and dependent on the object (the anaclitic) although I am not sure that it is so. For the acceptance in the other of a *jouissance* of another type can be lived on the narcissistic level as well as on the object-related one—since I can feel a narcissistic satisfaction in realizing that the other has a *jouissance* different from mine and that I am being completed by the other.

Is all love narcissistic?

Of course. And all investments (cathexes) of other behaviors are in great part narcissistic investments. This is part of Freud's discovery. Narcissism wants appropriation, and it is always then that there are difficulties between people, for each person is many people, not just the possibility of a double.

Is woman the double for a man?

A man can experience the woman as his double. But that doesn't mean that she is that. If you ask the question objectively, I would say no. But there is a psychological level at which one sees the other as a double, even if not exclusively so.

Do you agree with Freud that women are more narcissistic than men?

No, in general no.

Is it the opposite?

No. There are men who are more narcissistic than women and also women who are more narcissistic than men. I don't know what Freud founded this assertion on. Since he was not stupid, he must have touched on something. One speaks about his phallocentrism, which is one way of reading Freud. I think that there are other possible readings, and with different times come different readings. It might be superficial to call him—as one could also call Lacan—phallocentric. But I also think that both tend to be phallocentric in their theories.

One should consider if there is a more essentially feminine narcissism even though it can sometimes be found in a man, and if a particular type of narcissism can be assigned to men. I think that, for Freud, an explanation lies in the different development of the boy and the girl. The first love object for the girl is the mother, as it is for the boy. He doesn't have to change, but she must do so, according to the heterosexual evolution as it is described by Freud. Therefore, it is because the Oedipus complex is lived differently that there are consequences on the level of narcissism.

Do you think that if men and women would bring up children together equally, a lot of difficulties would disappear?

I see that that's what is happening in the United States. It also happens sometimes in France in different milieux. I don't know if this comes from the United States or if it is a movement which is developing in parallel ways in several countries. I don't think that it can level the difficulties, whatever they are. I even tend to think that it may complicate the problems.

Why?

It is difficult to interpret from a psychoanalytic perspective something that occurs on the sociological level and belongs to the evolution of customs. Each generation reacts in connection to the preceding one, trying to adopt a type of behavior which is supposed to solve the problems it is faced with. For example, it was a fact that everywhere in the West, following the interpretations and misinterpretations of Freud's thought, parents became less authoritarian, much more permissive. From the point of view of analytic practice, having been able to see it from where I am, which is a particular place, I would say that this has not simplified children's lives at all. On the contrary. I think that, in spite of everything, it is more structuring for a child to have to confront a contestable authority than to have to face the absence of authority. It is much more difficult to build up an identity in a very permissive climate than in a climate that has certain restrictions. And I think that, even if paternal authority in certain epochs has been a caricature, this had the virtue of making operative certain principles on the social level, in relation to which the child in its development could position itself, oppose itself, and find itself more easily. In a couple, the traditional roles of the father and the mother may become too undifferentiated or not differentiated enough. Now either one of them can take care of the baby, change its diapers, give it the bottle. Therefore there is a tendency to mask the differentiation in traditional parental roles, which was bound to the idea of what the man's and the woman's roles were supposed to be. I recognize that all that was perfectly arbitrary, and in a way contestable. Don't think that I want to say that the man should be the one who works outside the house and does not take care of the baby, while the woman ought to stay at home and take care of the baby. I don't have a preconceived idea about this. But on the other hand, a certain tendency toward the indifferentiation of roles has to bring to children who are brought up in this context supplementary problems with regard to the formation of their sexual identity, the representations that they are able to have of both sexes in relation to where they situate themselves, structure themselves, and differentiate.

I have a general view of this which may seem, at first sight, to be against progress; but I wouldn't want you to hear it in that sense because it is not at all what I want to say. I have seen these additional problems in analytic practice. I am thinking about analysands for whom this has created profound anxiety. The complication must be examined on another level. For example, in analysis I see a young husband of the type you were referring to. There is a true rivalry between him and his wife with regard to caretaking. They argue constantly because he thinks that the wife should not hold the bottle in a certain way, and that he does it better than she does. And the contrary may also exist, where both parents agree on the manner of feeding. I think that this may introduce a sort of mirroring between father and mother. Here the interchange of their roles may complicate the life of the child, for one image is not answered by a different image. It presents problems when he is not completed in relation to one of the two parents, when there is no exterior pole of reference, for example, if the mother is in a certain type of narcissistic relation to the child. To return to the question of narcissism, I think that when Freud says the woman is more narcissistic, it is very much bound to this question of the narcissistic relationship that she may have with the child. In this context, the father should be very different from the mother in his attitudes, behavior, ways of being. He would constitute at the same time a third pole of reference which isn't simply a replica or a double of the mother, but a different image of someone through whom there is a greater space for differentiation. In relation to images, he may be one thing or the other but not the same. For me, difficulty occurs when the images of men and women are too similar.

Can one change the symbolic order?
I think I know what is behind your question. A certain branch of the feminist movement might aim at what Freud would have called a return to matriarchy. Rightly or wrongly, Freud considered that the passage to patriarchy within history was progress. This could be disputed. If you like, I think that what belongs to Law, to the Symbolic, is more differentiated in patriarchal societies. That doesn't mean that the role of men is superior to that of women. Not at all. It is in this sense that feminism has posed excellent

questions and has caused society to change. Concerning the questions posed by Freud or those posed by feminism, society always has a tendency to go too far and to caricaturize, in a way, the answers that these questions might have brought. For example, sexual liberation as it has been practiced is a caricature of Freud, for Freud's discoveries do not lead at all to sexual liberation in the sense that was understood in the second half of the twentieth century.

Nor do I think that the questions posed by feminism ought to lead necessarily to the idea that the shared tasks of the father and the mother ought to be exactly the same, symmetrical and equal. I don't think that equality between men and women in their relationship belongs to the fact that they carry out exactly the same tasks. That's not necessarily equality. There will always be tasks that are done more easily by women. This doesn't prevent the possibility of equality between the two sexes, however. The egalitarian relationship lies much more in the way a man and a woman treat each other, without any domination by virtue of the fact that one is a man and one is a woman. There is no superiority in being a woman or a man in the relationship between the sexes.

In the United States, feminist analysts believe that it would be possible to deny sexual difference without falling into psychosis, an idea that is totally opposed in France. Doesn't the idea of sexual difference inherit the passion with which one had to separate from the Other in infancy? And isn't this first separation also a sexual separation?
This is in fact the heart of the question. I think that there are two completely different separations, that of the self and that of the Other. It is in this context that we speak of narcissistic choice rather than object choice. One of the great mysteries is how, departing from a kind of absolute narcissism, the child shapes itself, since at the beginning there is a sort of indifferentiation between mother and child for the infant. And how can the Other appear independently of sexual difference? These two questions are inseparable, even if there is a relation between members of the same sex, let's say the little girl and the mother. The question of procreation, which is: How does it happen that I exist rather than not exist? will of necessity bring

the question of sexual difference. Therefore there is self and Other only in connection with sexual difference. I can only *be* if sexual difference exists, and I can only be the Other if there is otherness and sexual difference. So the whole world of representations is built up from there. I don't know how one could arbitrarily isolate the question of the Other. That seems to me to create a split that does not correspond to reality.

If reproduction is ever taken out of the body, which it may be some day, would that change the whole constellation?
This is a very important question for the twenty-first century. Here, we can only hypothesize. However, I think that, on the model of the questions which have been posed in the course of history, we will attempt today, in the twentieth, and in the twentieth-first centuries, to resolve problems by technique, technology in the largest sense of the term. Technology has always existed since the origin of man. But let's talk about the development without precedent of technology and the capacity to construct the artificial reproduction of children in a purely artificial environment that we are probably going to arrive at quickly. I think that this is a way of liberating man in the generic sense of the term, from the precarious conditions in which reproduction occurs, in order to make it more independent in relation to natural reproduction and whatever that entails. But although some women have a strong wish not to bear a child, there are others who absolutely want this. I don't think that the future of humanity necessarily entails artificial reproduction.

We wonder if the stress on sexual differences does not depend on reproductive differences, however. If reproduction does become artificial, the sexual difference may no longer be that important.
I totally agree with you, and this has already begun. The sexual difference will become much less important, and probably, during a certain period of history, it will evolve differently. There are prototypes of androgyny, such as Michael Jackson, and humanity is going to experience this valorization of sexual indifferentiation, of bisexuality, for a while, by women as well as men. This is a way of trying to resolve the problem of sexual difference. Unhappily, this has negative psychological consequences which are not negligible. I

tend to think that all that is happening through the techniques of communication, the connection of man to the machine holds equally here, and that we are entering into an era that is a little schizophrenic. But this is an opinion that is hypothetical, and history works to give the lie to hypotheses of this type.

We have the feeling that the mythology of women is still alive and well today, particularly among the Lacanians and the Freudians.
You are right. In that way there is a side which is conservative enough in the Freudian revolution. But at the same time I don't know what would constitute progress for humanity.

Feminists like Simone de Beauvoir want women to be demystified. We think that mystification is very much alive in traditional psychoanalysis.
But how would you define this prevalent myth of women?

The eternal feminine. But what is the eternal feminine?
For me that is relatively independent of the evolution of society. I think that there is something which is able to modify itself naturally to the extent that the image of the mother and the woman are able to evolve themselves in the course of centuries. But I don't think that one can ever eliminate from the psyche the infant's fantasy that one keeps all one's life, which corresponds to this myth. Since it is a myth, it is different, but there is something real in society that corresponds to our representation. Perhaps this social reality could attenuate itself and disappear. But in my view it is not certain that it doesn't re-form itself constantly to the extent that there is an image, a representation that one can't eliminate because it is, in spite of everything, that of the infant, and even if there were artificial reproduction, the caretaker of the infant would always become the object of a representation of this type.

If Freud is right, this would be tied to the prohibition of incest, which insures that there will always be an image of the mother which will be like that of the nonsexualized woman. This doesn't prevent there also being a sexualized image of the mother. There are two representations, a split, the fundamental division of the subject without which there wouldn't be a problem.

Do women have a split representation of men similar to the split that men have of women?
Much less so.

Is this difference linked to differences in desire of men and women?
Exactly. And this brings us back to what we were talking about just before, with regard to heterosexuality. The little girl goes from the image of the woman to that of the man—the split occurs in this sense—while the little boy has to go from the image of the mother to the whore. Therefore there are two images of woman, one desexualized and the other sexualized. He has to make these two images fit the same person. When everything goes well, it's like that. But all the cases of impotence, of sexual difficulties, are bound to this split between the two images concerning the same love object.

That still exists?
Ooh la la. It's crazy to say that everything has changed. What one calls sexual liberation has changed nothing, and I would even say that it is more caricatural. There are enormous sexual difficulties for men and for women and moreover for love today. That's why I tend to think that there is something which pertains more to the psychic functioning *per se*, independent of the functioning of society. It doesn't matter if society changes and evolves, there is also a singular trajectory of each person who, at base, is always the same, whatever the society may be. Society cannot save anybody from the economy of this trajectory.

To return to literature, what are the similarities between the analyst, the writer, and the critic?
This is very vast. There is a whole history of the relations between psychoanalysis, literature, and literary criticism. There are different questions posed

on this subject in the United States and France. The literary critic considers the Freudian discovery in a different way in France and in the United States. It is a very complex question.

In your papers on literature, we noticed that you have avoided the kind of reductionism that so much psychoanalytic criticism falls into. We are trying to discover your secret.

It is rather simple. It is true that I avoid what has been called the psychoanalytic tendency applied in a reductive, hermeneutic manner the way Marie Bonaparte did with Edgar Allan Poe, which is nonetheless not without interest. In France, structuralist criticism followed. Then came the criticism inspired by Derrida's deconstruction, which is still more in favor in the United States than in France. Deconstructionist criticism is also marked by psychoanalysis because Derrida has always had a dialogue with it: questioning psychoanalysis and being questioned by it. There is a certain type of analysis that I do that might approach this way of reading a text, but at the same time, my principal concern is linked with that of Freud: to find in literature certain answers to questions that we pose to ourselves in psychoanalysis. If you will, in a way, it is the reverse of the application of psychoanalysis to literature. I try to discover in literature answers to questions that I ask in psychoanalysis. But at the same time, it is not a simple return to this Freudian question that someone like Marie Bonaparte, at the time of Freud, might have asked. It can only be a return which takes into consideration the evolution of literary criticism—Lacan, Derrida, and a few others.

If today I read "The Purloined Letter" by Poe, it won't be to discover either in Poe or in "The Purloined Letter" something that the most evolved theoretical analytic schemes could show, but rather to try to see better those questions which haven't been resolved in successive readings. For instance, the place of the interpreter in the interpretation: why Lacan identifies the analyst's place with Dupin's, why he does not take into consideration the inversion of signs in Dupin's identification of the letter, why the role of the double is neglected, and so on. Poe's text continues to be enigmatic, beyond a system in which one has wanted him to say certain things. I think that his text is inexhaustible. In great authors like Poe and Shakespeare, the genius of their writing is that one can never take a position of control which allows us to say, "Here is the entire meaning of the text," because the structure of the text is such that the reader is assigned to different places, and there is therefore an almost infinite possibility of readings.

What do you think is the most important question in psychoanalysis today?

One of the things that I consider very important is to renew its language, which implies that it reconsider all the models it has used, those of biology, physics, mathematics, along with Lacan. I think that the evolution of analytic thought will depend very much on its capacity to renew its language and not to reproduce purely and simply the models that have served it at certain times, even if it is still a young science. There is a tendency in psychoanalysis, which is a little embarrassing, that fixes us for a while in a certain language, whether it be Freudian or Lacanian. I think that Freud as well as Lacan ten or twenty years later wouldn't have expressed themselves as they did, that Freud would have reconsidered the relation of psychoanalysis and biology, for example. One of the fundamental problems is the capacity of psychoanalysis to renew itself in its connection with other disciplines, such as arts and literature, to renew its readings and therefore its language.

Isn't this what Lacan did?

Yes, but what I mean to say is that one cannot stop and, even within the work of Lacan, the way of posing the questions may change from one period to another. The problem is that students tend to rigidify, to fix thought, to want to conserve, to sacralize and dogmatize it, while the great thinkers are much freer, putting themselves more into question. They are always ready to reformulate what they have already formulated.

Selected Bibliography

Books:

Rêver l'autre. Paris: Aubier, 1977.

L'agonie du jour. Paris: Aubier, 1979.

Le discernement. Paris: Aubier, 1984.

Lacan avec Derrida. Paris: Mentha, 1991.

Articles:

"The Revolution of Hysteria." In *International Journal of Psychoanalysis*, vol. 55 (1974).

"The Language of Interpretation." In *International Review of Psychoanalysis,* vol. 1 (1974).

"The Logical Process of Interpretation." In *International Review of Psychoanalysis,* vol. 7 (1980).

"The Voice behind the Mirror." In *International Review of Psychoanalysis*, vol. 15 (1988).

With Patrick Miller. "Empathy, Antipathy and Telepathy in the Analytic Process." In *Empathy II.* New York: The Analytic Press, 1984.

"Reason from the Unconscious." In *The Oxford Literary Review*, vol. 12 (1990).

"The Parable of the Purloined Letter: The Direction of the Cure and its Telling." In *Stanford Literary Review* (Fall 1991).

nine

Béla Grunberger

with Comments by
Janine Chasseguet-Smirgel

What brought you to psychoanalysis?

BG I arrived in Germany, where I was a student in chemistry. As a foreigner, there was no place for me in the labs, so I spent a lot of time in the library, particularly in the periodical room. Among the reviews I found a psychoanalytic review in German, which I began to read with much interest. Then I started to read Jung, who is very readable, and finally I got to Freud and all the others. And that's how I began to be interested in psychoanalysis. From that moment I wanted to be analyzed, but it wasn't easy. Where I was in Germany there were no analysts, and then I had to leave Germany. I went to Switzerland where I studied economics and other social sciences and worked in a press agency. In Zurich, I went to the Burghözli where I followed Bleuler's case presentations.

JCS My husband left Switzerland in the first days of the war to enlist in the French army, but people were suspicious of him. They thought he was an espionage agent. He was put in a camp for foreigners—anti-Nazi Germans, Spaniards who were Republicans (that is, anti-Franco); then he left the camp *in extremis,* fearing that he would be handed over to the Nazis because he was Jewish. He was in hiding during the entire war and studied clandestinely in Grenoble and Lyons in the faculty of medicine, without having the right to take the exams, which was forbidden to Jews.

BG I studied medicine because at that time one had to be a medical doctor to be a psychoanalyst. This is not the case now. And afterward I started my analysis.

Who are your patients? Do you have mainly men or women?
BG It has always been pretty even, as in nature.

Where do you place yourself in the psychoanalytic movement?
BG With Freud, Ferenczi, the Hungarians first and then the Germans, the English Freudians. I am a classical analyst who is concerned with biology and works close to the body.

You have written on narcissism. Could you define your conception of narcissism for us?
BG I start with the hypothesis that the human being lives in certain conditions before being born and that the desire to recreate those conditions throughout one's life is commonplace. Before birth, a person lives in circumstances that constitute narcissism in the postnatal state: there is the desire to be unique the way one is unique in the womb, the desire to have no desire, where all is given; the desire to be sovereign, independent, and, above all, omnipotent the way one is in the womb, with a certain perfection which is a kind of ideal, which exists to a certain extent before birth, but which is complicated after birth by frustration. Narcissism is, first of all, not wanting to recognize this. Afterward, it is wanting to recover the same situation through drives, and living one's life with the illusion that this prenatal, ideal state can be found again in life or after life. This leads to different solutions, different ideologies, religions, and utopias to realize this ideal. All regressive means, such as addiction, alcohol, and love, also make one think that one can live in a state of absolute perfection, the way one imagines it exists either in a prenatal state or in heaven. I see narcissism that way. But there are all sorts of narcissisms. There is a narcissism which is always frustrated, which leads to a very bad temper. There is narcissism which is

lived in solitude; another type which exists in crowds. That is, narcissism is sometimes nourished by an image that is at the heart of an illusion that we share, which may create mystics, sects. In fact, there are all sorts of positive or negative manifestations of this idea of recovering a lost perfection.

How is your concept of narcissism different from Freud's?

BG Above all, Freud conceived of narcissism as a pathology, because he discovered it along with mental illness, hypochondria, schizophrenia, paranoia. He saw narcissism in certain types of women.

JCS He sees it in criminals, the great felines, children, and women.

BG Not all women but a category of women, the women whom he compares to cats. That is, the type of woman who has need of no one, who finds her happiness in herself. The great criminals fit into my theory perfectly. They correspond completely to the conditions of the prenatal. They know no authority and do what they want. In my book on narcissism, I wrote that I tried to analyze a man who killed his father. I went to see him in the psychiatric hospital where he asked what I wanted. I said that I wanted to analyze him. "Why?" So that he could change, I said. "Me? I'll never change in my life. I'm fine the way I am." "But you killed your father." "It was the happiest day of my life."

One hears a lot about primary narcissism. Would you talk about the other types?

BG Classically, secondary narcissism involves an object and an identification with it. Primary narcissism is something innate and more than innate since I speak about its existence before birth. (However, in Freud there is more than one definition of primary narcissism.)

JCS I think that one important difference between narcissism as Freud conceives it and as my husband does is the hypothesis that narcissism comes from prenatal life. Freud spoke only one time, and then in passing, of this prenatal narcissism. Another important difference is that he considers narcissism not as a simple direction of the drives, but as a force *per se*, often in opposition to the drives. My husband has also insisted on the positive aspects of narcissism, in particular, at the heart of the analytic cure. For him, narcissism is a driving force for the cure. At the time this was revolutionary because my husband showed that the patient makes a narcissistic regression when he enters analysis and that he hopes to recover that narcissism through the cure. Basically, there is a narcissistic illusion that underlies the desire to be analyzed. If it were only that, one would reach an impasse, but there is always this which is in the background. This caused a scandal in France when he spoke about it because people only believed in the negative aspect of narcissism. Freud never considered narcissism as an aid for the cure. On the contrary.

BG I consider narcissism as the locomotive of the cure. First one needs a narcissism which can accept a change because there is also a narcissism that doesn't accept any change. There is also a narcissism that is opposed to analysis because, as was the case with the criminal, the person considers himself "fine," as he said. And even if he isn't happy, he can take medication but certainly not have analysis. What's necessary is an analysand who is sufficiently narcissistic to regress but not too narcissistic to undergo analysis, which is a sort of demystification of narcissism. Gradually what one can do with interventions is to interpret something that the patient has, up to that moment, frozen in consciousness, which was a more or less illusory construct. All the defenses that one uses naturally reveal themselves to be illusory and disappear after having been duly interpreted. Therefore, in analysis, each interpretation can be considered as a giving up of narcissistic illusion and the acceptance of a piece of reality. Each time a little more. At the end of an analysis, there is a reconciliation between narcissism and the drives which integrate the ego; the two together finish by leading—ideally—to a synthesis. At that moment the narcissism becomes something normal because there is always narcissism that the individual needs to love himself and to give himself value, even more than he deserves. This is delusion, but it is necessary in order to live.

Could you speak about the ego ideal in relation to narcissism?
BG The ego ideal is narcissism as agency.

Mme Chasseguet-Smirgel writes of the ego ideal as an avatar of narcissism.
BG An *avatar* means to appear in life in another guise. Certainly I consider

it this way since it becomes an agent like the superego for morality. In one of my articles, I emphasized a double track in the psyche: One track with desire, superego, castration, guilt, and another with narcissism, frustration, and shame. It is always necessary to see the two tracks as separated to understand our conflictual life and dreams. It is necessary to establish what belongs to shame and what belongs to guilt, for example.

Is nostalgia for the narcissistic stage stronger among men or women?

BG Tiresias was punished because, after having been a woman, he said that women have nine times more sexual pleasure than men, according to his experience. The gods blinded him, but gave him the gift of inner sight and prophecy. Ultimately, in analysis, sexuality is important. But what really counts is something beyond or below sexuality, something very profound: narcissism, pure happiness.

JCS But which gender is more nostalgic for such narcissism?

BG One might say that women care more about it. Men are more "drive-oriented." But you can't generalize. There are individuals—men and women—who sacrifice life itself, for example, the melancholiacs, through suicide, because, according to me, they seek another resolution, which aims at pure narcissism. One finds the type that prefers the narcissistic solution above all in men, for example those who flung themselves into martyrdom at the beginning of Christianity.

JCS But isn't this tied up with the idea that I suggested, that a woman can find this narcissistic regression more easily than a man through her ability to be a mother? In pregnancy there is a fusion in which the mother can totally identify herself with the fetus that she carries. And this is something that men do not have. And to go back to your answer, men satisfy this nostalgia by other means.

BG Women are supposed to be more idealistic than men. But they are also more pragmatic, probably because of this physiological factor.

Might we consider narcissism to be the foundation of all desire?

BG Desire has an instinctual origin. But to have one's desire triumph in a satisfying fashion and in a way that is flattering for the personality is the domain of narcissism. The components of narcissism vary. Some seek brutal satisfactions for their instinctual desires. Others reveal more refinement and sensitivity in their narcissistic exigencies.

Dr. Hyman Spotniz, in the United States, has proposed a theory of negative narcissism, which consists of a devaluation of the self and the valorization of the object.

BG It is a type of narcissism that is no longer narcissism because it has been displaced. It is the contrary of narcissism. Narcissism is, by definition, love of the self. Evidently there is narcissism in love, but there is above all the object of love. One can also love someone through narcissism; that is, by identification. There are couples who love because of resemblances. There is also the contrary, where one loves through complementarity. But the wish is still narcissistic in essence: to be complete.

Do we have more and more of a narcissistic personality in our time?

BG Certainly, but for negative reasons.

Which ones?

BG Degradation of the object, lack of maturity in the bond with others. An impoverishment rather than an enrichment which turns one toward the self because one cannot turn to the other. It is a pathological narcissism which is not truly a love of the self. It is because there is nothing else that one goes back to one's own self. But this narcissism actually is immaturity, and it is because there is this immaturity that the young seek drugs and perversion. It is a search for a fictitious happiness, which results in a chemical change and not one in the personality of the individual. Through a bad interpretation of Freudian thought, we have arrived at a moment of general laxity in education which keeps the young in an immature state.

JCS With laxity and also the destruction of the family, education has suffered. One also finds the too conventional family. But one has not found something better for the development of the child than the family.

BG We see a rejection of the world of the father. A general rejection. And then we are in the aggressive situation of the world of the primitive mother. That is a theory that should be developed.

In Europe, it seems that the sexual is the great difference. In the United States, there is a current position which seems to hold that the sexual difference is not essential. Our question is whether the idea of sexual difference inherits the passion with which the child separates from the mother or whether that separation is the difference itself?

BG You say that in the United States one can deny sexual difference? And that in France sexual difference is a fundamental difference in identity and in psychological life. Yes. A nondifferentiation would lead to psychic death. My wife wrote a book on perversion in which she shows that the negation of the sexual difference and the difference between generations is basically the negation of reality. These are the two bedrocks of reality.

To go back to the separation from the mother, is the separation between me and the other also a sexual separation?

BG It is a separation if one is a boy.

JCS It is also a separation if one is a girl. You sound like Stoller.

Would you please explain?

JCS Stoller says that it is easier for women to acquire their sexual identity because they don't have to differentiate themselves from their mother, whereas with boys there is this phenomenon which he describes as an imprint of the mother on the son, which causes him a lot of trouble in acquiring his sexual identity, for he has to make a great effort at undoing fusion. Although his discoveries are remarkable, I don't think that this is entirely true.

It seems to me that the woman's sexual identity has to be achieved also. It's achieved through opposition to the mother, with the possibility of the girl's integrating her identification with the father. A woman is not simply the feminine. A woman is also a being who is doubly sexed and who therefore has an identification with both parents. And you [to Grunberger] in analysis also insist very much on the necessary identification of the woman with her father and not only with her mother.

BG Certainly, both parents are involved. However, a boy identifies more easily with the father than the mother. It is necessary to do both. I think that the big question is something that has not been worked on very much yet. That is, to arrive at maturity, the two sexes have to introject the paternal phallus to arrive at personal independence.

JCS My husband considers the identification with the father and the desire to have a penis as a normal phase of feminine sexuality, which it is necessary to integrate.

BG This is what I call the introjection of the paternal phallus. This is why I said that this is an advantage for women in its complementarity. But women also have a problem. Because this introjection must pass through a phase. We have said that the woman is idealistic, narcissistic. For her the anal aggressive introjection is a more important conflict than for the male. I think that this is her essential problem because it is an introjection that she sometimes doesn't accept because of its anal component.

One often hears that sexual perversion is more common among men. Do you agree?

BG I have a conception of perversion that holds that one can be perverse without showing it. This is why women seem to be less perverse. I was just speaking of the anal introjection of the phallus. For men, most perversions are anal. In general, one considers the perversions to be anal, for example, sadism, masochism, coprophilia. But there are other perversions which do not seem to be perversions because they are not anal but which nonetheless for me correspond to the definition of perversion. That is, a sexual satisfaction that is regressive and obtained like a little baby's, for example, through the different contacts of sexual mucous as in kissing. In perversion, there is the contact of sexual mucous which corresponds to the contact of the uterine mucous by the fetus. It is a way of reliving with a man or a woman the prenatal contact with the uterine mucous and also the amniotic fluid. This is a very thick liquid that contains a lot of organic material and excrement and has an odor.

Do these perversions exist in men as well as in women?

BG Yes. But men in general have perversions that are more overtly anal.

Lesbians are not that way. The lesbian couple is mostly the mother and child.

We have noticed that the woman is somewhat mutilated in the psychoanalytic literature in that she has no breasts. The breast that is mentioned is only for nourishment. But as sexual organs, breasts exist very little. They become the breast and not breasts.
BG No.
JCS That's totally true. Have you ever read an article in which the breasts are treated as a sexual organ?
BG Yet all the time in clinical observations patients say that they are attracted by breasts.
JCS But that's on the couch.

Our question relates to the psychoanalytic literature.
JCS That is so. There is the breast of the mother. And that's it. One never speaks of the sexual organs that the breasts represent and of the fact that *for women* the breasts are an important erotogenic zone.

We return to the question. There is nothing about menstruation or pregnancy in the psychoanalytic literature, nothing about loss of virginity either. Menopause does not exist. All these things are important events in a woman's life. Where is the woman in the psychoanalytic literature?
BG If you go to the *Bibliothèque Nationale*, ask for the Hindu psychoanalytic reviews written forty years ago. There was a very strong psychoanalytic movement in India then. All the Hindu psychoanalytic literature of that time deals with menstruation.
JCS Well, but with this Freudian sacred theory of castration, bleeding women are castrated women. Menstruation is never positive. One only considers it when women stop menstruating or when they have a disfunctioning for pathological reasons. One has to consider the anguish that this provokes. Menstruation does not represent the fact of being castrated to women. It represents the fact of functioning as a woman. If a woman dreams of menstruating, some men as well as women analysts are still able to interpret this as castration.

BG But not me. To menstruate is to be a woman. (Silence.) And the breasts play a very great role. They are sexual organs for men and for women. Above all for men.

JCS Ah. But why above all for men?

BG A woman does not need her breasts or those of another woman to enjoy sex while a man needs a woman's breasts.

JCS Come on now. Sexually, a woman's breasts play a very important role for her. And if she is homosexual her breasts and her partner's breasts are essential. It's true that one never speaks of them. It is perhaps because of their appearance later in life, in connection with puberty.

The breasts are a very important erogenous zone that exists in pornography. Men like pornography. Women don't seem to.

BG Because it is something anal. Women are afraid of anality. Women refuse the anal structure of the phallic introjection in general.

JCS There is fragmentation also in pornography, not the total object. This fragmentation is essentially sadistic.

BG I would say that it is mainly connected with immaturity.

As for the part object, it would seem that there is no greater part object than the phallus. Is that a fragmentation?

BG It's a part object but it is also a total object. A woman, for some men, is a phallus in the unconscious.

Is the archaic mother always phallic?

BG No. Although she can be. The archaic mother can sometimes be the good mother and sometimes the bad.

Does this mean that the bad mother is phallic and that the good one isn't?

BG Perhaps we should not put it that way. The good mother is narcissistic-oral, while the bad one is mainly anal-sadistic.

Is it the bad mother and not the good archaic mother who is sexual?

BG The good mother is sexual, of course. Otherwise she isn't a mother. What defines a mother is that she is of the female sex. But the sexuality of the mother involves dealing with many conflicts. But above all she functions as a loving and enveloping mother.

But the virgin is a mother who isn't sexual.

BG Exactly. She is the virgin mother from whom sexuality has been removed, and hence the relationship with her is no longer conflictual.

JCS But making her nonsexual eliminates the father above all.

BG Eliminates the father yes, but this also makes him a narcissistic being, a god who is asexual. In the Christian religion, there is no sex.

JCS Therefore there is a desire to have a nonsexual mother?

BG Certainly. It is at the same time a castration because she has a phallus, which is, at the same time, Christ. She is always with him. The mother and the child.

You have written about religion and the mother. Patriarchal religion seems to forget the mother. But in truth the mother is within it. Would you develop this more?

BG It is the religion of the family. When one says family, one means the mother and the child, and the father certainly, even in religions that only recognize the mother because at one time there were only matriarchal religions with only goddesses. The gods did not exist. But all the same, in the background there is God the father, who among the Christians is found exiled to heaven. But he exists all the same. Above all there is guilt in religion—and sin. Sin is castration of the father, the desire to castrate the father, which is always there. The great guilt of original sin is castration, the castration of the father, even if he only exists as a shadow without a third dimension.

What is the relation between the castration of the father and circumcision?

BG Circumcision is a problem that is very much discussed. I just spoke about perversion. I think that the idea behind removing the foreskin is removing perversion. There is a very interesting article by Masud Khan which describes a case involving fetishism of the foreskin. That is a perversion, and it is this perversion which is eliminated when the foreskin is removed.

JCS This question is very interesting. It seems to me that it is connected to your first article on masochism, where you describe a masochistic mechanism, which is tied to the need to show that the son is not castrating the father, but rather that it is the mother who castrates the father in the primal scene, for example, or that one is castrated oneself. This latter is the most common defense, leading to all sorts of masochistic behavior, trying to say to the superego, "Look at me. I am castrated. I am not the one who castrates."

BG In circumcision there is this demonstration: I am not the one who has castrated the father. Besides if one thinks of the story of Moses, God wanted to kill him because he had not been circumcised, but his wife circumcised him at the last moment with a big stone. One finds this guilt with regard to the father who wants to punish.

Lacan speaks about Moses and circumcision.

BG Yes. About Moses who was already old.

Much has been said about Lacan's own narcissism in relation to his phallocentric theory. Why did Lacan have such a great influence in France? Even among women?

BG Although he was very antifeminist. He was a misogynist.

JCS You could briefly tell the story of Lacan asking you to come and see him.

BG In 1953 there was a schism. Lacan left the Paris Psychoanalytic Society.

JCS In 1963, the International Psychoanalytic Association said to those who were with Lacan: We would recognize you but you have to separate from Lacan. And then he asked you to come to see him.

BG He invited me to his home for a glass of champagne. He wanted me to join him. I told him that I wanted to remain in the Paris Society. His wife put out a bottle of champagne and left. He said to me, "Oh women!" with such scorn. It had an obvious homosexual flavor, and his charisma had to do with that. At that time, not many women followed him, and they were not welcomed. But Lacan always got people through his words. In his seminar there were hundreds of people who listened to him for hours. They came expressly for that—as if for a Mass. Often they didn't understand (as with a Mass in Latin) but he was a charismatic man, seeming to show something and hiding it at the same time—a wonderful magic phallus.

Is the phallus a way of hiding misery (*un cache misère?*) for Lacan?
JCS The question touches on the narcissism and phallocentrism of Lacan and his success.
BG The penis is the contrary of narcissism. But the phallus is a narcissistic symbol in the unconscious. The notion of narcissistic completion is represented in the unconscious by the phallus. Very often the story of castration is above all a narcissistic castration. And the fear of castration is a fear of narcissistic castration. In dreams one sees this very well because as an image there is only the phallus. And it is necessary to know for interpretation if it's narcissistic or anal/sexual.

When a woman criticizes the theory of phallocentrism, people accuse her of penis envy. You give another interpretation. This is very important for a book about women.
JCS I think that you have seen women who have spoken on this question. There are also men who envy women's capacity for maternity. This is something very important and should be analyzed. It's necessary to know how to look at it. One has to hear it. Psychoanalysis is not an exact science. The personality of the analyst plays a very important role. He hears what he wants to hear—only to a certain extent, hopefully.

There is also penis envy among men.
BG Certainly.

As for the amorous state, love, there is an idealization that is compromised by the difficulties of daily life. Do men and women react differently to the degradation of the amorous state?
BG True love is something which is a composite, where there is a little of everything. And there is above all a lot. I thought I would have a lot to say about this with you because you are dealing with the analysis of women by

men. And I would have to say that there is no difference (on this point) between men and women because analysis is carried out in a certain dimension of the psyche which is asexual. And in true love there is that also. That is, there is a narcissistic dimension which is asexual in itself. And that is very important in love. I would also like to say that an analysis, in which the material is apparently always sexed, is in fact carried out in an asexual dimension that I call the monad. Because I think that the infant at birth keeps a bond with what one might consider an externalized uterus, something like this relation continues to exist. And this monad is also very important in love. It develops and evolves. It is just like the relation in an analysis. (There is a monad, that is, a deep asexual bond.)

Who are the great narcissistic characters—especially women—in literature?

BG All of them. Among men, Don Quixote, Don Juan.

JCS Among women, that depends. Why did you say all? There is Emma Bovary.

BG That is a pathological narcissism. There is Karamozov's woman, Grushenka.

There is Anna Karenina.

JCS There is Célimène.

BG With Célimène, it is the man who is more the narcissist.

In what category do you put Félicité in "Un Coeur Simple" and also Mother Courage? Is Isolde narcissistic?

BG You are giving us a lot to think about with your questions. Isolde has a great capacity for love. There is in love something which again reveals regression. I think that it has to do with a prenatal regression, which means that love is always connected to death. There is suicide, certainly, and also one dies easily in love. In *Romeo and Juliet* both of them run to death. One always thinks that something will save them. The grandeur of love is in its ending. Love is against life, and one has to explain it by death. One flings aside all the materiality of life.

JCS In *La Princesse de Clèves,* the lover, the duke, is ready to sacrifice himself for love. He is ready to sacrifice himself, but at the same time this is a very narcissistic state.

BG There is a way of being satisfied with one's narcissistic completion to the point that one cannot accept life as it is afterwards. And at that moment one might kill oneself, kill oneself through narcissistic exaltation.

The troubadours wrote about a faraway object.

BG In courtly love, one loves the woman but one doesn't come near her. The lovers can be separated by a thousand miles. Petrarch lived far away from Laura.

Dante wrote about a woman who was dead. You can't get any further away than that.

Selected Bibliography

Narcissism: Psychoanalytic Essays (1971). New York: IUP, 1979; second ed. 1992.

New Essays on Narcissism. London: Free Association Books, 1988.

Authors Cited

Chasseguet-Smirgel, Janine. *Sexuality and Mind: The Role of the Father and the Mother in the Psyche*. New York: New York University Press, 1986.

———. *The Ego Ideal: A Psycoanalytic Essay on the Malady of the Ideal*. New York: W.W. Norton, 1985.

———. *Creativity and Perversion*. New York: W.W. Norton, 1984.

———. In Elaine Hoffman Baruch and Lucienne J. Serrano. *Women Analyze Women: In France, England, and the United States*. New York: New York University Press, 1988, pp. 107-126.

Khan, Masoud. "Foreskin Fetishism and its Relation to Ego Pathology in a Male Homosexual." *International Journal of Psychoanalysis* 46 (1965): 64-80.

Spotnitz, Hyman, and Phyllis Meadow. *Treatment of the Narcissistic Neuroses.* New York: Manhattan Center for Advanced Pschoanalytic Studies, 1976.

Stoller, Robert. *Sex and Gender.* New York: Jason Aronson, 1968.

———. *Presentations of Gender.* New Haven: Yale Univerisity Press, 1985.

ten

Otto Kernberg

Differences:
Psychoanalytic Theory and Culture
in France and the United States

We know that you have been influenced by such French analysts as Janine Chasseguet-Smirgel, Joyce McDougall, André Green, Michel Fain, and Denise Braunschweig. What in their theories has given you the most insight into sexual difference?
Well, I don't think that there is one single element, but to begin with, French psychoanalysts have been exploring the nature of the erotic much more systematically than analysts in other countries. It is true that in recent years there have been important contributions in the United States as well, for example, by Ethel Person and Martin Bergmann; they have written interesting books about love. But there is no doubt that there is a much more systematic, older, complex literature coming from France. In a strange way, the beginning of that was Lacan's view that the shadow of the father falls in the separation of the symbiotic relation between infant and mother, initiating separation together with sexual differentiation. This view of the archaic Oedipus complex that has been elaborated in different ways by Chasseguet-Smirgel, Laplanche, and many other writers, is an interesting and I think very helpful development of Freud's thinking about original bisexuality.

Of course, many of the authors who have influenced me most have been very critical of Lacan's views, particularly of his later views, and even more so of his technique, but in reacting against Lacan, they have in turn developed the theory further in ways that I found very interesting. For example, Braunschweig and Fain describe a differentiated reaction of Mother toward the infant, according to whether it is the same gender or a different gender from Mother. And it makes eminent sense to me, observing women while they are pregnant and after having their babies, that there is an intense erotic relationship to the baby from the beginning. Laplanche says that the messages that Mother emits have an erotic quality that the baby is not yet able to understand but experiences as enigmatic, and out of these enigmatic messages come the original fantasies of seduction as well as the original fantasies of the primal scene and castration. So there is a linkage of the main anxieties of the Oedipal situation starting very early in life and determining the respective psychology of men and women.

It seems to me, in terms of my clinical experience, that such a differentiated relationship between mothers and infants of both genders is certainly observable. There has also been observation that shows that the attitude of the mother toward the infant changes when the father is present. Now, I think that all of this, from a psychoanalytic viewpoint, has something to do with the unconscious identification of the infant, not only with Mother, but with Mother and Father, the unconscious assumption of their relationship, and the gradual buildup of a sense of closeness with Mother that eliminates Father temporarily. When Mother returns to be an adult woman with Father, this creates a teasing quality of excitement and rejection in the relationship between Mother and infant and opens up and triggers the development of sexual desire, together with the unconscious identification with Mother and with being the object of Mother's desire.

Now, this is different for a little boy and a little girl in the sense that Mother tends to, subtly and unconsciously, I think, inhibit the primary vaginal genitality of the little girl, except if she has a homosexual attachment to the little girl that dominates over her heterosexual impulses. But in the case of the little girl, the wish to be loved by Mother then triggers fantasies of being Mother's love object as well, and therefore an identification with Father that then shifts into longing for Father, given that the normal erotic attitude is more distant from Father to the little girl. So it seems to me that some subtle normal erotic rejection of Mother, together with fostering the identification of the little girl with her, including the identification with Mother's erotic attraction to Father, combine to facilitate the move of the little girl toward Father, and create the particular eroticism of the little girl which is an eroticism of distance, a more diffuse eroticism. The primary vaginal genitality is inhibited, at the same time that there is a capacity for relationship in depth with the other gender earlier than that of the little boy because the intense ambivalence towards the mother is left behind in the search for an ideal relationship with Father. Trusting in such a relationship from a distance is what Fain and Braunschweig call the courageous step of the little girl. This leads me to propose that the little girl develops her capacity for object relations in depth earlier; her capacity for genital enjoyment develops later because she has to reencounter it in the context of an object relation in her adolescence. Little boys, on the contrary, are highly stimulated erotically, genitally stimulated, while their ambivalent relation to Mother takes much more time to be resolved into a capacity for relationship in depth with women. Little boys become genitally free first, and are eventually able to establish an object relation in depth. Little girls have the opposite road.[1]

Well, all of this, I think, stems largely from my reading of French authors. From Joyce McDougall, I take the stress on the importance of polymorphous-perverse infantile sexuality enriching sexual life. From Chasseguet-Smirgel, I take the characteristics of the archaic Oedipus complex and the normal narcissistic conflicts of the little boy who is not up to being the object of desire to Mother. These have been very helpful contributions.

I have been interested also in Donald Meltzer's proposal that early ambivalence toward the infant's mother stems from the idealization of the surface of Mother's body while projecting aggression onto the interior. This leads to both the idealizing, erotic, exhibitionistic, voyeuristic, sensual quality of body surface contact, and to the aggressive implications of penetration and being penetrated that are part of the erotic response. The integration of aggressive elements into the erotic response I take from Stoller's work. It fits very well with my observations of conflicts in the sexual life of couples.

These are the body of influences that I have tried to put together in my writings about this subject. My book on normal and pathological love relations is forthcoming with Yale University Press.[Ed. note: The book is now published. See bibliography.]

How do you account for the enormous influence of Lacan on French psychoanalysis?

Well, first of all he was an extremely brilliant man who had a charismatic quality, and who presented French psychoanalysis with a new, direct reading of Freud. And without a good reliable translation of Freud into French at that point, he had a kind of monopoly. He also had important original contributions: the mirror stage, the conceptualization of the Imaginary and Symbolic spheres of experience, the archaic Oedipal complex, his questioning of linear models of development, focusing instead on the simultaneity of diachronic and synchronic development, his combination of the use of structuralism, the cultural effects of surrealism, and the anti-American spirit of French culture. He combined philosophical, political, and original psychoanalytic formulations and aroused an important response in that culture in the same way that psychoanalysis, with its more adaptational, optimistic, sociological approach, as presented by ego psychology in the United States in the 1940s and 1950s, also aroused a cultural response. Of course you might say, to the contrary, that psychoanalysis was influenced by the culture to develop in different directions, so that there was a kind of dialectic interaction between culture and psychoanalysis. In a way, his changes in technique—the shortened psychoanalytic hour, the shortened training—facilitated a rapid and great reproduction of psychoanalysts, in contrast to the more difficult, lengthy, arduous, and rigidified training at more traditional institutes. So there were cultural factors, political factors, and factors regarding psychoanalytic education, even economic factors, in terms of how long it takes and how much it costs to have psychoanalytic training.

Lacan was a brilliant and original man, who unfortunately also had a charismatic and demagogic quality that created a kind of a religious spirit around him. As I read Lacan, particularly the late Lacan, there is a lot of mystification and illustration of the irrationality of the unconscious by irrationality of exposure. And that is really mystifying, although also attractive. But he served an important purpose, and interestingly enough, what I call the French mainstream (the other authors we have mentioned), starting from their rejecting some of his thinking, were able to contribute many original points. Some formal Lacanians who are not yet really part of the International Psychoanalytic Association but whose influence is growing illustrate the richness of his thinking, as well as its problems and limitations. I am thinking, for example, of Piera Aulagnier and her contribution to the theory of psychosis, and of François Roustang and his critique of the rigidity of Lacanian psychoanalytic education, which is an important critique of all psychoanalytic education. And of course, major theoreticians, such as André Green, who has contributed so importantly to our analysis of narcissism and borderline conditions and in a way was influenced by, although he was very critical of, Lacan. In fact, André Green's important contribution to the study of affect theory was in reaction to Lacan's neglect of affect theory. The unconscious is not simply structured like a language. The unconscious has something to do with deep affective dispositions that Lacan did not consider. There were, of course, also other political influences. Marxist theoreticians picked up some of Lacan's thinking to complement Marxist theory with a psychoanalytic theory: the unconscious identification with Father represented by the capitalist regime. Althusser picked up Lacan and introduced psychoanalysis into certain French Marxist thinking. These were additional influences.

What did Lacan bring to American and South American psychoanalysis?

To American psychoanalysis relatively little. The influence of Lacan in this country is mostly in intellectual circles, not directly related to psychoanalysis as a therapeutic enterprise—departments of history, French, English literature, art—but in the helping professions there is little influence of Lacan, because it is very different from the traditional, empirical, highly rational thinking prevalent in American psychology and psychiatry. In Latin America, on the other hand, Lacan has been much more influential, because Latin American culture is also more oriented toward French culture. And the greater concern with cultural and philosophical issues on the part of

Lacanian-oriented psychoanalysis has a resonance in similar interests on the part of Latin American psychoanalysts, who are much more interested in applying psychoanalysis in the study of local tradition, culture. Latin America is noted for its present concern with its cultural background and definition. In general, the Lacanian influence has been strong in the Latin countries, both in Europe and in Latin America, much less so in the Anglo Saxon and Germanic cultures of Northern Europe and North America.

I think there are probably many linkages between general cultural dispositions and the acceptance of certain psychoanalytic theories. For example, I don't think it's a coincidence that Self psychology has had its major appeal in this country because it is an optimistic, environment-oriented form of psychoanalysis that is in contrast to the more pessimistic, skeptical focus and the unavoidability of aggression that you find in classical psychoanalysis, which appeals more to other cultures.

What do you see as Lacan's greatest limitation?

Well, first of all the mystifying language. Second, more concretely, his theory of the unconscious, which neglects the central importance of affective aspects of the unconscious. The unconscious is not simply structured like a language, although that sounds very catchy. Third, lack of sufficient consideration of psychic structure, characterological structure, and their implications for the organization of unconscious conflicts. His focus was mostly on the expression of the unconscious and unconscious conflicts through language; Lacanian technique is highly influenced by the focus on language, on "nodal points," in which the unconscious emerges. And it is true that for healthier patients the communication of subjective experience by means of language is essential, but for sicker patients, nonverbal manifestations, characterological patterns that are revealed in nonverbal behavior, and the enactment in the transference and countertransference are relatively more important than simply the content of free associations. You have to open up your total field of vision to the nonverbal and to systematic analysis of dominant relationships in the transference and countertransference. I think that is neglected in Lacanian writing. In general, there is very little about psychoanalytic technique, very little about the clinical, and much philosophical speculation. As you listen concretely to the clinical work of Lacanians who have stayed as such, there is a certain chaos regarding their technique which I find troubling. These are the main criticisms.

Lacan believed that the child's entrance into language marks his or her entrance into the "male" Symbolic order, but doesn't the mother play a major role in introducing the child to language, a role that Lacan seems to ignore?

Of course. The Symbolic order is not simply a male-supported order, and reason and rationality are not simply given by the Oedipal father, but by the Oedipal couple. And in this regard, there is a tendency in Lacanian thinking to see the mother exclusively as the mother of symbiosis, the mother of fusion, the mother of the Imaginary, while the father is seen as the principle of logic, external reality, the law. I think that to some extent this reflects the psychology, if you will, of a paternalistic culture, but not a psychological reality. In this regard, Chasseguet-Smirgel particularly has pointed out, I think very reasonably, that there is an Oedipal mother, not only the symbiotic, pre-Oedipal mother, and that the principles of rationality and logic come from both parents. Lacan has been feeding into a certain cultural cliché that the law is the law of the father. It's the law of the Oedipal couple, of the parents who see themselves as a couple, affirming their joint structure in life, that is, an eminently rational quality which lays down the law of separation of sexes and generations and sexes, and it doesn't come only from father. The problem with Lacanian thinking is that sometimes ideas are presented almost as slogans, whereas the clinical realities are much more complicated.

Does the great emphasis on the father in Lacan represent a wish for the father that no longer exists, that perhaps never existed, or hasn't existed for a long time?

Well, the wish for order, rationality, predictability, is one of the most positive aspects of the human mind. Ego psychology and adaptation have a role, if you will, to enter into a reasonable social contract, but that cannot be linked only to the role of the father. This is really, I think, a remnant of paternalistic tradition. Some of this can even be found in Freud, although

Freud, within the limits of his own culture, was going as far as he could to oppose the conventionalisms of his day by raising questions about the sexual purity and innocence of women.

In contrast to France, the most influential theory in the United States and Britain has been that of object relations. Could you briefly define its salient points?

I would define it as a broad spectrum of psychoanalytic theories that have in common the assumption that the earliest internalization is of significant relations with others—internalization not of an identification with an object but rather of a relationship—so that in all interactions what we internalize is the role relationship of the two persons who interact, the dyadic relationship. The infant in relating to Mother internalizes not only the image of Mother, but the image of self as relating to Mother. So there is a simultaneous buildup of a self-representation, an object representation, and an affect linking them. The basic units of intrapsychic experience are: self-representations, object representations, and affects linking them. And I think these are the building blocks out of which eventually the tripartite structure of the ego, the superego, and id are built.

And of course this internalized structure is influenced by later object relations, so that there is a reciprocal relationship between earlier internalizing experiences, their structuralization, and their enactment later on in treatment and in all other relationships. This is the common aspect of theory linking Melanie Klein, Fairbairn, Winnicott, Balint in Britain, and Erik Erikson, Edith Jacobson, Margaret Mahler, and also Harry Stack Sullivan in this country. So object-relations theory crosses the entire spectrum from culturalists—what we used to call culturalists but are now called interpersonal psychoanalysts—to Kleinian psychoanalysts.

You have made major contributions to the theory of narcissism, a subject that greatly interests French analysts. How do you define narcissism? Do you distinguish between positive and negative narcissism?

André Green distinguishes between a *narcissisme de vie* and *narcissisme de mort*. Narcissism in the simplest terms can be defined at a metapsychological level and at a clinical level. At the metapsychological level, it is the investment of libido in the self and the regulation of that investment—its vicissitudes and consequences. There is also a very primitive narcissism which is linked more to aggression than to libido, namely in which the protection from pain, trauma, and danger is achieved by self-elimination, a profound temptation to self-dissolve, to disappear. To deny or destroy the awareness of one's own existence is an aspect of severe depressions and psychosomatic disorders. This is André Green's contribution.

Now, from a clinical viewpoint, I would say that narcissism is the regulation of self-esteem and deals with all the structural determinants of self-esteem regulation, including both the quantitative increase or decrease of self-esteem and the extent to which there is a sense of an integrated self in contrast to a dispersed self. Normal self-esteem includes both the sense of an integrated self and normal gratifying self-regard, pleasure in one's existence, in one's relationships and activities. Regulation of self-esteem depends on structural conditions of the psychic apparatus. It depends first on the integration of the self-concept, second on the dominance of libidinal over aggressive investments. Here the clinical merges into the metapsychological. It depends on the integration of the normal superego and the protective ego ideal, the extent to which the ego ideal functions are dominant over self-punitive functions. Self-esteem depends on the gratification of basic impulses, on an ego structure that facilitates the gratification of aggressive and libidinal impulses. Dominantly, it depends on the internalization of integrated representations of others, and relationships between self and object representations in the internal world, which create an internal world of gratifying relationships that protect the individual against aloneness, loneliness, loss of self-esteem, and permit survival under conditions of external frustration and nongratification.

From that viewpoint, one may classify the pathology of narcissism into certain types or levels. First, we have normal narcissism, normal self-esteem, regulated by all the features that I have mentioned, and a normal adult value system integrated in the superego, with learning in many areas of the ego and superego, so there is a realistic self-criticism, but not a tendency to react with excessive guilt or fluctuation of self-esteem. That would be normal narcissism.

In infantile narcissism, characteristic of most neuroses and character pathology, all these structures are intact but are fixated at the level of infantile functioning so that the content of the superego is determined by infantile assumptions. For example, here, self-esteem depends on being clean, on not having sexual impulses, or on the neurotic inhibition of particular impulses. In all neurotic and characterological symptoms, there is a narcissistic component, in the sense that the forbidden impulse cannot be expressed, for it would lead to a reduction in self-esteem or self-regard because of guilt or shame.

There are rare cases in which the self is identified with an object predominantly while the self-concept is projected onto an object. Certain cases of male homosexuality, especially as described by Freud, in which a man loves somebody else because that other person stands for himself, represent narcissistic love in contrast to normal love. In this connection, normal love relationships always combine object libidinal and narcissistic features. In other words, the difference between narcissism and object libido disappears in a normal love relationship.

And then, finally, there is the most severe type of narcissistic pathology, in which instead of a normal self there is a pathological, grandiose self, involving a narcissistic personality having to do with profound structural alterations in early childhood. The integration of all the real and idealized aspects of self and object representations and ideal self and ideal representations forms a pathological structure, while all negative aspects of self and of internalized object representations are repressed, projected, dissociated, the effect being a pathological grandiose self with an impoverishment of the world of internalized object relations that exist in the case of normal narcissism. There is weakness of superego integration so that the supportive functions of the superego are missing, internalized relationships with others are missing, and this grandiose self depends on external admiration to maintain the boundaries. Here we have the narcissistic personality.

Is narcissism in women the same as it is in men?
Structurally I see no difference. In clinical practice we find as many narcissistic personalities in women as in men.

But not more?

Not more. Women with narcissistic personalities struggle with gr___ envy than neurotic women because the conflicts between the sexes do not derive only from Oedipal competitiveness but now acquire a profound narcissistic quality as well. In the narcissistic personality, there is often a sense of intense envy toward the other sex. I would say regularly. Equally strong in both sexes.

So there is womb envy in the narcissistic male?
Not necessarily womb envy in a strict sense. Envy of women and of all female functions, in the sense that not being both sexes at the same time is a narcissistic insult. There is also an intense and unconscious envy of Mother, at the origin of the envy of women. In both narcissistic men and women there is an intense envy of Mother which in the case of men is directly expressed as conscious and unconscious resentment of women.

In women, the envy is secondarily displaced from Mother to Father, so that the primary envy of Mother becomes a secondary penis envy, which reinforces penis envy extraordinarily and therefore makes narcissistic pathology in women clinically almost more difficult to treat.

One of the French analysts that we interviewed said that all love is narcissistic. How do *you* define romantic love?
I don't know that I can define romantic love really, but I would say that a romantic dimension is part of the normal love relationship insofar as it implies an idealization of the other person and of the relationship, an idealization that I don't see as a defensive process, but as a normal development, an enactment of the values of the ego ideal, which are expressed at three levels. One is the level of the sexual encounter, the idealization of the body of the beloved and the idealization of the sexual relationship itself, which I think is a fundamental aspect of the capacity to love. Now, I am talking only about sexual love; I'm not talking about maternal love and friendship. Second, at the level of object relations there is an idealization of the relationship with the other person as a source of love received and as the recipient of love, which has much to do with the achievement of what the Kleinians call the depressive position, the capacity to integrate aggression and love with a dominance of love with which to repair the aggressive

aspects of all intimate relations, which is expressed as tenderness and the wish for closeness and fusion in the love relationship. And third, an idealization at what you might call the superego or ego ideal level in which the other person stands for what one wants to achieve in life. There is an idealization of the new reality created by the couple that realizes in external reality the interpersonal, the intrapsychic ideals that derive from the ego ideal. The combination of these three dimensions creates the romantic dimension of love.

That's not the whole story because if the loving aspects at all three levels jointly constitute an idealization, there is a counterpart to this: the aggressive activation at all these three levels, the unavoidability of ambivalence in human relationships and therefore the need to accept that in all emotional intimacy, such ambivalence will come up in the form of intense activation of aggression so that the ideal is consistently threatened by its opposite. That trust and love will dominate over hatred is a hope and expectation, but there is an aggressive dynamics that enters into romanticism as well.

Now, stepping back, I am very interested in Georges Bataille's analysis of eroticism and his classifying human relationships into (a) ordinary work relationships as rationally controlled and dominated by the boundaries of space and time, and (b) the ecstatic extremes of both love and hatred that disrupt daily life again and again and create a dialectic with it that can never be resolved. The erotic dimension, for him, is precisely this dialectic between, shall we say, the Dionysian aspects of human relations as opposed to the Apollonian, and I think that in psychoanalytic terms it has to do precisely with these travels between idealization and its counterpart, the integration of the dialectic with aggression that gets activated in intimacy. That's how I would put it together. I'm condensing things as much as I can.

Would you say such love is the same for both sexes?
Yes. But as I have already discussed, the road to it varies.

In an essay called "The Conquistador in the Dark Continent," Carol Gilligan wrote that "the language of the object relations analysts in general with its borders and boundaries creates an imagery of love which is indistinguishable from the imagery of

war." Should love be separated from the imagery of warfare? Certainly, such imagery existed traditionally, in the poems of Petrarch, for example.

Well, she goes from metaphor to theory. I guess that's legitimate, although not really scientific in a strict sense, but I would say that from a conceptual viewpoint, love and war are intimately mixed. Love and hatred cannot be separate. The psychology of pure love is an illusion. It's naïveté.

Is there any way of overcoming that double standard of aging whereby youthfulness in a woman seems to be far more attractive to men than youth in a man is to women?

I think Chasseguet-Smirgel has either written about this or commented personally to me that behind this problem is the greater fear of ambivalence in relation to Mother on the part of men. An older woman signifies Mother, and her aging signifies the death or destruction of her from the inside, which has to do with the projection of unconscious aggressive impulses into the interior of Mother's body. Donald Melzer's theory, which I referred to before, speaks of the idealization of the surface of Mother's body by both genders, and the projection of severe aggression into the inside of her body. I think that the psychological determinants plus the cultural biases and demographic reality cause this difference.

But there has been some change. Younger men and older women—we do see that to some extent.

Yes, I agree. Insofar as social biases and strict control over what is acceptable behavior change, this may shift. On the other hand, I am a pessimist, insofar as this difference derives from childhood fears. The little girl, wanting to be loved by Father, accepts a dependent relationship with him. This dependent relation to the Oedipal object is in contrast to the little boy's fear that his little penis is not satisfactory to big Mama. Chasseguet-Smirgel has written about this very significantly. I think this may be one more psychological reason why men are afraid of older women, and this translates into a social bias. Social bias resorts in part to the massive collective projection of infantile superego function. The conventional part of us—what we say is the right thing to do—is much more determined by unconscious, infantile superego factors than by conscious reasoning. As individuals we are mature and have our individual morality. But when we submerge ourselves in group processes, conventionality takes over, created by our own collective unconscious, and this is a dialectic from which it is hard to escape.

Will the "new father" and his increased contact with the infant lead to a new idealization of the father's body?

I don't think that the amount of time spent would change fundamentally the unconscious identifications. It seems to me that if the father carries out all the mothering functions with the infant, his relationship to the little girl and the little boy would be different and would stimulate separation from the boy and an erotic quality in the relation with the little girl. Now you might say that would intensify further erotic longings for Father in the little girl. But there are some basic biological functions that would still be heavily preempted by Mother, so that the shift in the amount of time spent is probably not going to change these basic psychological attitudes. Mother would still feed the baby, and as society gets more civilized, the right and need for women to spend relatively more time than fathers with the baby is still going to be recognized. I know there is a movement that says both fathers and mothers should have equal time but I think that it is partly ideologically motivated, more of a fashion than a long-term trend.

We have to separate what look like revolutions on the surface from long-term changes. There is a kind of oscillating pattern as you look into the history of gender relations over an extended period of time. I have no doubt that there is going to be an increase in the at-least-two-jobs-per-family situation, in other words, that women will continue to increase their very large participation in work and all functions outside the home. But I believe that it is likely that a certain differentiation of functions will persist, particularly when it comes to nursing and the earliest development of the child. So I don't know whether that is really going to create basic differences. In the same way, you know, the question was raised of what will happen to little children who are brought up by homosexual parents. There is already some evidence that their sexual development is perfectly normal. So long as they don't become homosexual objects to their homosexual parents, it is surprising how normal their development can be. I am talking about the work of Martha Kirkpatrick and others in this regard. Social functions and roles and even the nature of the sexual relationship between the parents on the conscious level are not enough, I think, to overshadow the deep unconscious linkages. By the same token, a woman who is heterosexual, manifestly, but with a profound hatred and dislike of men, will communicate that rejection of the little boy's sexuality without being aware of it. Although she may not be consciously homosexual, unconsciously, serious disturbances may occur because of the rejection of the little boy's genitalia.

How is one's choice of heterosexuality or homosexuality determined?

Freud made it very clear that usually people have a dominant orientation, and that it's very hard to change that. People are dominantly homosexual or dominantly heterosexual, usually. Now we know that it is not so simple. I think that there is a psychological bisexuality that is universal. But rapidly the orientation tends to crystallize around the homosexual or the heterosexual orientation in terms of object choice.

Do you think that this is a biological determination?

We don't have good empirical evidence, but you have to differentiate four aspects of sexual behavior: the intensity of sexual excitement, the object of sexual desire, the identity of oneself, and behaviors that are linked to one's gender identity. These four components have different mechanisms, although they are all in a package in our sexual behavior. Intensity of sexual desire—we know we need normal biology and a normal hormonal level, and beyond that certain doses of androgens in both sexes, in both genders, to be able to have normal sexual response, but on top of this, it is a psychological fact that you can have normal biology, but with sexual inhibitions, the sexual response is gone. The biological apparatus has to be in place along with psychological freedom; for practical purposes the psychological determinants override by far the biological preconditions. Second, regarding core-gender identity, whether one is male or female, whether I feel male or female, is mostly decided by assignment: there is good evidence for that. Third, general behavior patterns that are seen as masculine or feminine are mostly determined by the culture, only some hormonally, which means genetically. Lastly, whether one is interested in somebody of the same gender or the opposite gender, we have no research on because of our taboos against infantile sexuality. And those taboos against infantile sexuality are as strong and alive as in the time of Freud. To think of children as sexually innocent is so dear to our hearts that it's part of the outrage about the sexual abuse of children. Children are seen as innocent with no sexual impulses. This is particularly strong in this country, which is a very puritanical culture, much more so than France. There is a taboo on the study of children's sexuality which is interfering with knowledge, so we don't really have very good direct evidence. We have indirect evidence that shows that male homosexuality is influenced by social, cultural factors. There also are cases where it seems to be influenced by genetic factors. So it is reasonable to assume that it is a complementary series, but what John Money calls one's "lovemap" is constructed mostly out of psychological factors, secondarily out of genetic, or constitutional factors. I think this is a reasonable way to put it at this time. We need more evidence. Given the fact that there is a psychological bisexuality anyhow, we all have the potential of being, let me say, switched on in both directions. Women are less afraid of homosexual relations than men. This is very clear. But we don't know whether this is due to cultural influences—paternalistic cultures are dead set against male homosexual sexuality, while they tolerate female homosexuality—or whether it is due to primary identification of the little girl with Mother that strengthens her sexual identity and makes her less afraid of homosexual relations. It is an open question. But my assumption is that there is a combination of genetic and psychological factors, and that the psychological factors that determine homosexuality are by far more important. That's clinical; again, all of this is now ideologically questioned. Homosexuals say it is all genetic, but we have to separate the ideology from scientific development, which is really in a very early stage. I refer you to the work of Richard Friedman in this country, who is probably the most interesting researcher in this field dealing with the question in a nonideological way.

Do you consider homosexuality a perversion or an alternate lifestyle?
I think that it is an open, very complex issue, in which the last word has not

yet been said. I start out from the psychological bisexuality that I mentioned earlier, and from that viewpoint, homosexual longing and experiences are universal. Second, I think that, insofar as homosexual urges are part of polymorphous-perverse infantile sexuality, they are part of the perverse capabilities or potential of the human being. These impulses enter not only into sexual foreplay but into sexual eroticism in the broadest sense, and the inhibition of polymorphous-perverse sexuality, including homosexuality, sadomasochism, exhibitionism, and voyeurism, leads to a decrease in the capacity for erotic excitement and gratification in sex. This is a most general statement.

From that viewpoint, one would assume that there is a capacity for homosexual excitement and experience in both genders. It is part of the capacity for sadistic and masochistic, and voyeuristic and exhibitionistic tendencies. In theory, if homosexual inclinations and other inclinations were part and parcel of an essentially heterosexual orientation, that would make theoretical sense. But it doesn't happen like this in practice. Homosexual behavior often becomes a dominant, exclusive orientation. The question is, does this make homosexuality the same as all other perversions? I would say no, because from the start, in a homosexual relationship, there may be an integration of sex and tenderness, of all the components that we have in a heterosexual relationship, with an integration of all other partial components.

Have French analysts contributed to your thinking about homosexuality?

There is an argument given by French psychoanalysts, precisely by Chasseguet-Smirgel and Joyce McDougall, that after the normal overcoming of conflicts, the identification with the Oedipal parents also implies the identification with the reproductive functions of the parents. By definition, homosexuality means renunciation of paternity or maternity. That's a good point, an interesting point. Of course, it could be argued that very often homosexuals still want to be parents to children and that parental functions that many homosexuals carry out are perfectly normal. I think there is very good evidence for that, as Martha Kirkpatrick has demonstrated.

Would you explain the difference between core-gender identity

and social-role identity, which are important concepts in the United States?

Because of Stoller and other researchers, we now know that core-gender identity is determined by the gender identity assigned to the child by the parent. That is a fundamental confirmation, I think, of psychoanalytic theory, in the sense of the extreme importance of an unconscious relationship between the sexes in determining what you feel and who attracts you. We have evidence that whether one feels a man or a woman is determined by the assignment of core-gender identity. Gender-role identity—I'm using the terms *core-gender identity* and *gender-role identity* following other authors, particularly Ethel Person—is much more flexible. What is considered masculine and feminine changes from culture to culture. In the Renaissance, for men to be explosive, emotional, dependent was considered perfectly manly. This is different in contemporary Anglo-Saxon culture. These are socially determined roles, and these could obviously change. But core-gender identity, I think, is determined by a deeper level of relationship.

From this viewpoint, I have a question about Stoller's hypothesis that feminine identity is stronger than male identity because of an original identification of both genders with Mother. He has some good arguments for that. For example, the fact that women are much more comfortable with their homosexual feelings than men. Women can easily enter into a homosexual relationship, for example, in group sex. Men can do so only if they are dominantly homosexual. If not, they enter into sexual panic. But we have to consider how powerful social forces operate against male homosexuality and much less against female homosexuality. So I think that while there are observations that support Stoller, there are also arguments against him, and in short, I believe that there is no such primary identification with Mother in both genders, and that Mother from the beginning establishes an erotically reciprocal relationship with the little boy, while there is a tendency to much more neutral identification with the little girl.

Wouldn't the sexual inhibition of the little girl disappear if the father were there taking care of her more?

Yes, possibly that would be an important difference. Of course, one might argue that, insofar as the Oedipal temptations would be much stronger, the Oedipal prohibitions would be much stronger also.

But then wouldn't both sexes have similar patterns of development?
In the sense that if Father took care of the little boy, the little boy's identity with Father would be stronger. But then one could say that perhaps the little boy's prohibitions toward Mother might be stronger too, since there would now be a double loyalty toward Father. I think there might be significant changes, but I don't know in what direction. In any case, fundamental differences between the sexes would persist because of the differential attitudes of both parents toward the genitals. From this viewpoint, I see again the nature of unconscious identification as much more important than the quantity of contact, and I would separate core-gender identity from social-role identity.

There are a number of clichés in this area. For example, the assumption that women are more dependent and look for closeness and that men look for independence—you know what Carol Gilligan says. I think that this is ideology, and I'm not very interested in that. It deals with the social-role-identity issue. From a psychoanalytic viewpoint, it's less relevant.

Is it possible to see the analytic cure itself as a reenactment of the "courageous step" of the little girl, in that it repeats both the experience of fusion and separation?
Yes, for both genders, of course.

Is there a danger that the male analyst might keep the woman patient from separating? Some French analysts are now speaking of the danger of female patients being seduced by the male analyst, with whom they may remain in treatment for as many as twenty or thirty years. What is or should be the place of the male analyst for the woman on the couch? It seems to us that women analysts are far less prone to either seduce or be seduced

than are male analysts.
Seduced in what sense? Erotically, to have sex with patients? Is that what you mean?

One analyst spoke to us about women patients who feel that the only one who listens to them is their analyst, and not being able to separate because of their need for this. That's one of the seductions of the analyst. Another would be sexual, yes.

Another well-known analyst that we interviewed in Paris spoke of the temptation that the male analyst might have for conquest, for a certain kind of violence toward the female patient, in an attempt to prove a certain machismo, which he had to be extremely conscious of. This would of course depend on the good analysis of the analyst.

Sexual seduction of patients is unfortunately very frequent in this country; perhaps up to thirteen percent of all therapists are guilty. Fortunately this figure is much lower among psychoanalysts because psychoanalysts are trained to understand this, to deal with the countertransference. Once again, one has to guard against cultural clichés that describe males as having a certain psychology and women as having a certain psychology. If Freud's concept of unconscious bisexuality is of any value, and I think it is, then both male and female analysts, as well as all males and females, have feminine and masculine aspects of their personality. I am very suspicious of the description of typical female psychology, and male psychology, as if males have male psychology and females have female psychology because there are unconscious identifications in both genders. Now let me add a number of additional concepts before we talk about one aspect that I am about to mention. In the nature of the erotic relationship in the transference and countertransference, there is the gender of the patient, the gender of the therapist and the nature of the psychopathology. Neurotic women in treatment with male analysts develop typically intense, positive Oedipal fantasies and desires, with intense eroticization of the transference at certain moments, and therefore also unconscious attempts to seduce the analyst, which may correspond to unresolved problems in the psychoanalyst (mostly narcissistic pathology in the male analyst) that may lead to mutual seduction.

Narcissistic women in analysis with male analysts don't develop strong erotic attachment. They have enormous resistances against that, because to be erotically related means to be dependent, which is anathema to the narcissistic defensive structure. So you have very little eroticization in the treatment of narcissistic women by male analysts except if they have strong antisocial features, because then the effort to seduce the analyst is a way to corrupt the analyst and the analytic situation, which is typical of all patients who have severe antisocial features.

Now, if you have a neurotic male patient in analysis with a female analyst, the erotic attachment is relatively weak because of the sense of inferiority and insecurity of the little Oedipal boy toward the big Mother. So most of the erotic feeling expressed toward other objects is displaced. This does not mean that there are not some erotic feelings and wishes toward the female analyst, but this is much less frequent and intense than in the case of neurotic women with male analysts. Narcissistic males in analysis with female analysts, in contrast, develop intense erotization, with an aggressive implication of trying to seduce the female analyst, which again reinforces their sense of narcissistic power. Why the difference? Because the power gradient in culture is such that men seduce women, so that narcissistic males feel very happy seducing their analysts if they can. It's a defense against the dependency that they cannot tolerate, while for female narcissistic patients sexualization would express a dependency that would be shameful, as I said.

As you see, there is a cultural gradient. Little girl in love with big Daddy reinforces certain transferences. While the other cultural gradient, little boy in love with big Mother runs against the cultural tendency and therefore is inhibited in the psychoanalytic situation. But these are defensive formations that have to be analyzed eventually, and their analysis permits us to deepen the understanding of the Oedipal complex in both genders. So you see that the situation is quite complicated and cannot be reduced to a simple formula. Usually women with intense neurotization establish excessive erotic dependency because these are the healthier women; women with severe narcissistic problems don't tolerate any dependency. On the contrary, borderline women may establish long-term dependency, but it is not an erotic one; it is an intensely ambivalent and aggressive one. And the same is true for borderline male patients in analysis, who also establish very intense, dependent relationships. And in those cases, there is paradoxically much less difference in the way they react to men or women because at very regressed levels the analyst is treated very often as a combined Mother/Father figure. You see why I am objecting to the kind of simple formula that one finds once in a while.

We were surprised to find that in psychoanalytic theory masochism is a more prevalent perversion among males than among females.
Oh, all the statistics show that. All sexual perversions are more frequent in males than in females. There is no doubt about that, and this has been explained by the great prevalence of castration anxiety in males. Castration anxiety in women takes more diffuse forms of fear of bodily damage, in contrast to the concrete linkage to the genital organs of castration anxiety in the male. You also find perversions among women, but they are less frequent. In the case of women, it is much more built into the characterological structuring of the polymorphous-perverse tendency. In males, much more frequently there is a complete perversion. Masochistic masturbatory fantasies are probably more prevalent in women than in men, almost universally, but to have to experience pain to be able to achieve sexual orgasm is more frequent in men.

Is splitting of the sexual object by men, the Madonna/whore syndrome, still alive and well?
Yes. I think that a crucial problem in male psychology derives precisely from the issues that we discussed. In the normal uninterrupted development of genital erotic responsiveness, men, when they come to puberty and adolescence, have the capacity for sexual excitement and orgasm, and usually, except in the case of severe neurotic circumstances, they have masturbation with sexual fantasy. Although they suffer from the identification of all women with Mother, who is forbidden as a sexual object, the solution is to split women into idealized mothers and devalued whores with whom sexual life can be carried out very fully. I would consider this practically a normal development in puberty and early adolescence in men. Normally this is overcome in late adolescence and adulthood, but it may persist into adulthood.

Does splitting of the sexual object also occur in women?

Yes, particularly women with an hysterical personality structure, but it's less frequent. What is most frequent in women is an idealized, defensively dependent relationship to a man, with a sexual inhibition that only gradually can be overcome. The woman may jump into sexual liberation with another "forbidden" man so you have the same dichotomy, but it is a dichotomy that doesn't have the split aspect from the beginning. So you find it in both sexes, but more accentuated frequently, typically in men.

The Madonna/prostitute dissociation is characteristic of male adolescents. But there is also a kind of split in female adolescents, which is the joint idealization by a group of adolescents of an idealized effeminate male, a rock star or whatever, dissociated from a private, personalized, idealized, masochistic involvement with a secret, forbidden man. That's an equivalent—there are dissociations in both sexes. In the same way, male pornography has its equivalent in the Gothic romances of women. I don't know what you call them.

Harlequin romances, a very popular genre.

In your paper "Aggression and Love in the Relationship of the Couple," you write that both sexes "long for a complete fusion with the loved object, with Oedipal and pre-Oedipal implications that can never be fulfilled." Aren't men afraid of this fusion, unlike women, who seem to desire it?

I don't think so. Here we have the conventional cliché of men who don't dare to love. You see men who are terribly dependent, longing little children who desperately want to be taken care of by a woman, and very often women who get very afraid of such an overwhelming relationship. I find men as dependent, and striving with dependent impulses, as women. I do think that, in women, culturally dependent regression to an Oedipal relationship is fostered. For a woman to be a little-girl-woman is perfectly normal, approved. It's wonderful; that's how she should be, so that the regression is culturally processed. A man has to be independent and stand up, but this doesn't mean that psychologically he doesn't have any conflict. And very often it bears on the fact that men may take a mistress with whom they are little boys, and she is the good mommy who loves taking care of them.

And as you know, very often, men's mistresses are much older women who can be warm and giving, in contrast to their wives with whom they have to be the big macho man. This is as frequent as the men who take a little girl, so they can be big Daddy because they can't be that with their wives. I really think that these are conventional issues: that women are more dependent and men can't be dependent; or that men have more of an objective sense of justice. I think women have a clear, objective sense of justice too!

You have expressed admiration for French analysts who have been willing to take unpopular positions and to go against current ideology—with regard to feminism, for example. We would like to hear you say more about this.

You can find American analysts who run counter to what is fashionable and what is politically correct in the same way as French analysts. I think psychoanalysts outside their concrete work with patients are just ordinary human beings affected by their cultural backgrounds. The only thing that I would expect from a good analyst is to be nonconventional in the concrete situation with a patient, to be able to move outside ordinary conventional thinking. If a psychoanalyst cannot do that, then he really doesn't have a conviction about the profound, irrational forces influencing human behavior. But outside the psychoanalytic session, if he becomes a purely conventional individual, I don't mind that. It is almost unavoidable.

Is psychoanalysis as it is now practiced reductionist, elitist, too limited to those of European background? How should the treatment of minority patients, emigrés for example, differ (or should it) from the treatment of the middle and upper classes? In France there is a movement called ethnopsychiatry, which has been influenced by the work of Georges Devereux, who did work in this country also. Should there be such a movement here?

I don't know. I have had experience in analyzing patients from different cultures and different socioeconomic environments, and it seems to me that, while undoubtedly the analyst should become aware of the cultural background of the patient, and such awareness should color his interpretations, on the other hand, at a deep level we are all much more human than otherwise. If the analyst protects himself from the clichés in his culture about the other culture, again that is a way of being nonconventional. The analyst should be able to recognize such differences if they exist and learn about the other culture as the analyst analyzes what is going on with the patient. A simple example. The analyst sees a black patient in this culture. The black patient may feel inferiority with tremendous cultural and ideological backing. It is important for the white analyst to study that in terms of its cultural background and sort out from that what is a more personal transference. Now, if the analyst comes with a feeling of guilt and treats his black patient as special, the analyst is licked and the patient is licked. So the analyst has to step out of the cultural biases regarding blacks in the same way that the black patient will have to step out of his own biases regarding whites.

It struck us when we were doing research in France that so many psychoanalytic journals that we looked at were affiliated with universities. That is rarely the case in this country. We were wondering how we can get psychoanalysis into the university here the way it is in France.

This is a major problem. I think it has to do with a certain self-isolating quality of psychoanalytic training institutions in this country and the lack of sufficient attention to the development of psychoanalysis as a science, to research, which has given psychoanalytic education a certain dogmatic quality that alienated the university. There has been, on the one hand, in the past, an ivory tower attitude on the part of organized psychoanalysis and a rejection on the part of disappointed and critical university members. I believe that it is an important, unfinished task of psychoanalysis to reestablish strength and develop the relationship with both the university and the culture. I think that's basic, and there is a growing awareness of that within psychoanalytic circles in this country. Ten years ago, twenty years ago, the full-time psychoanalyst in private practice didn't do any university or hospital work—it was a matter of pride. Nowadays, the sense that psychoanalysts have a certain social role, that psychoanalysis needs to develop its scientific basis, that we have to support researchers who are psychoanalytically trained to work within a university setting, is growing. It's a problem in this country, but analysis is finally waking up to it and we're beginning to take action. Also, at the International Psychoanalytic Association there has been a growing interest in how to develop the scientific aspects of psychoanalysis to foster specialized research as well as an educational methodology which would be attractive to people who are getting university training.

Why are the French so much less concerned with whether psychoanalysis is considered a science than Americans seem to be? Well, in France the relationship between psychology and philosophy, psychology and the humanities, in general, is much stronger than in this country, and psychoanalysis within this general field is being developed in terms of its implications for psychology, sociology, philosophy, as well as the deeper understanding of the unconscious. That's the big plus for the French. In this country, I think the potential—to some extent actual—big plus is the interest in empirical research, in the effort to develop further psychoanalytic knowledge by applying to the study of psychoanalytic treatment some of the methods of scientific research coming from boundary disciplines. That is true for this country and also to some extent for the German-speaking and Scandinavian countries. I think that in Latin cultures the development of psychoanalytic thinking, the analysis of the nature of the unconscious as it emerges in clinical situations and can be applied to culture, is a main concern. They are suspicious of empirical research because they find it more geared toward the surface phenomena, toward actual behavior, not respecting the unconscious, in part naïve and limited. I believe that, in contrast, in this country there is a lot of critique of French psychoanalysis as speculative and not "scientific." I believe that both roads are important, that these are different avenues for developing psychoanalytic knowledge, so I am interested in both ways of progress, rather than simply saying one is opposed to the other.

Mythology, particularly the mythology of women, seems to be alive and well in France. For example, references to Antigone, Clytemnestra, and la femme fatale abound. This is not so in the United States. Has psychoanalysis here departed from its origins in the exploration of myth, and is this a problem, or are we creating a new mythology here?

It is true that psychoanalysis has been much less interested in mythology in the United States. But I think that this is part of the different orientation of psychoanalytic inquiry. The interest in mythology is part of the interest in history and cultural anthropologies strong in Latin countries and in Latin America, while in this country we are mostly interested in empirical research and applied psychoanalysis. The analysis of the psychoanalytic application to myth is a major interest in Latin America as part of the application of psychoanalysis to culture. I think that's the main issue, not that psychoanalysis has developed a different mythology in this country. The same is true for the application of psychoanalysis to literary analysis. I think it is much stronger in France than it is in this country, although it is developing here. And the relationship of psychoanalysis to political ideology is much stronger in Europe and Latin America than in this country.

Should psychoanalysis address the problems of the culture at large?

Very much so—with the cautionary note that psychoanalysis cannot pretend to have the instruments for universal knowledge. The application of psychoanalysis to the study of culture means honest interdisciplinary research, not what we have to teach the others, but the mutuality of learning between psychoanalysis and other fields that deal with cultural analysis: cultural anthropology, sociology, politics, history, literature, literary criticism. These are fields for mutual enrichment, so my answer is yes, but not in the sense of psychoanalysis pretending it has all the knowledge and all the answers.

What are the forces that are trying to close off insight, and why?

Insight means an awareness of the paradox that some of the creative forces are at the same time the destructive ones. This is painful and leads to denial and to simplification and an attempt to restore harmony. Such denial tends to decrease insight. That is obvious culturally.

Leaving psychoanalysis aside for a moment, if you think of our cultural ideal of liberty and equality, there is a profound contradiction between them. If everybody is free there will be inequality. If we make for absolute equality, freedom will be restricted. That is a conflict that has totally destroyed the Soviet Union. In different ways we are also struggling with it.

I am not comparing us to a society that is totally corrupt, but the problem is universal.

Speaking about liberty and the different definitions of equality we are subject to, what is your position on feminism, and what are the particular contributions to feminism that psychoanalysis has made?
I'm more impressed by French feminism than any other type, the humanistic approach of Simone de Beauvoir, for example.

For me, feminism is a very important approach to the social, political, and economic inferiority of women in all traditional societies, including those of the Western world. And I think that the feminist orientation of psychoanalysts who have pointed to limitations in Freud's thinking because of his identification with this culture is very important. Edith Jacobson pointed out that Freud's assumption that women have less of a superego than men is absurd. Edith Jacobson, Melanie Klein, and Clara Thompson, for example, raised questions about the biased views within traditional psychoanalysis without considering themselves feminists but contributing to what I think is potentially an important feminist psychoanalytic approach and for me really the position of Ethel Person and Martha Kirpatrick, Janine Chasseguet-Smirgel, and Joyce McDougall. I'm very much in line with their thinking.

I think psychoanalysis has made important contributions in pointing to some of the mutual fears and resentments of the genders, in helping to explain how cultural mechanisms and structures deal with such anxieties and fears. For example, the profound psychological fear of women against which paternalistic culture is a defense, the differential nature of conflicts that derive from cultural bias and structures in contrast to those derived from individual psychopathology, the separation of the awareness of objective oppression from women's masochistic tendencies, derived from an unconscious identification with the devaluation of women. The cultural reinforcement of sexual inhibition in women is part of traditional patriarchal cultures. The regressive forces in what can be called "Old Boys' Clubs" and "Old Girls' Clubs," in the sense of group phenomena, tend to separate the genders. Group culture interferes with the autonomy of the individual and of the couple. There are many complex aspects of psychoanalytic thinking that help to make feminism more sophisticated in a psychological way. On the other hand, of course, psychoanalysis can be transformed into feminist ideology, and again you have the problem of transforming psychoanalysis into a worldview. I find that extremely dangerous. I prefer that somebody be feminist and separately a psychoanalyst, that somebody be religious and separately a psychoanalyst, rather than condensing these. Because I see a risk of ideological condensation with psychoanalysis as a science. When psychoanalysis becomes "a conception of the world," whichever way you put it, psychoanalysis and socialism, psychoanalysis and Marxism, psychoanalysis and feminism, psychoanalysis and nationalism, I find this an extremely dangerous development because it tends to idealize psychoanalysis and eliminates the potential technical neutrality of the analyst and respect for the autonomy of the patient.

What do you see as the major question for psychoanalysis at this time?
The development of psychoanalysis as a science with a unique understanding of the structure of subjectivity, the development of psychoanalysis as one of the instruments for understanding our culture, the further development of psychoanalysis as a method of treatment and applications of this method of treatment, and the development of psychoanalytic education: these are the major tasks right now as I see them.

Note

[1] In our meetings with him, Dr. Kernberg also noted that differentiation in early development "has biological features as well, the externality of male genitals, the phenomenon of erection....Under ordinary conditions, the biologically hidden or interior qualities of female genitals get powerfully reinforced by the selective inhibition of genital eroticism in the mother/daughter relationship, which means that there is an inhibition of primary feminine genitality which has to be reencountered, and which only happens in puberty, but is fully in process already in infancy. We find infan-

tile masturbation in both sexes, but as we know, female masturbation that starts around seven-to-eleven months of age is inhibited rapidly by age eighteen months."

Selected Bibliography

Borderline Conditions and Pathological Narcissism. New York: Jason Aronson, 1975.

Object Relations Theory and Clinical Psychoanalysis. New York: Jason Aronson, 1976.

Internal World and External Reality: Object Relations Theory Applied. New York: Jason Aronson, 1980.

Severe Personality Disorders: Psychotherapeutic Strategies. New Haven: Yale University Press, 1984.

Psychodynamic Psychotherapy of Borderline Patients. New York: Basic Books, 1989. With M. Selzer, H.Koenigsberg, A. Carr, and A. Appelbaum.

Psychoanalysis Toward the Second Century. New Haven: Yale University Press, 1989. With Arnold Cooper and Ethel Person.

Aggression in Personality Disorders and Perversion. New Haven: Yale University Press, 1992.

Psychic Structure and Psychic Change. Madison: International Universities Press, 1993. With M. Horowitz and E. Weinshel.

Love Relations: Normality and Pathology. New Haven: Yale University Press, 1995.

Authors Cited

Aulagnier, Piera. *Un interprète en quête de sens.* Paris: Ramsay, 1986.

————. *Les destins du plaisir: aliénation, amour, passion.* Paris: Presses Universitaires de France, 1979.

Bergmann, Martin. *The Anatomy of Loving.* New York: Columbia University Press, 1987.

Balint, Michael. "On genital love." In *Primary Love and Psychoanalytic Technique.* London: Tavistock, 1959, pp. 109-120.

Bataille, Georges. *L'érotisme.* Paris: Minuit, 1957.

Bion, W.R. *Experiences in Groups and Other Papers.* New York: Basic Books, 1961.

Braunschweig, Denise and Fain, Michel. *Eros and Anteros.* Paris: Payot, 1971.

Chasseguet-Smirgel, Janine. *Female Sexuality.* Ann Arbor: University of Michigan Press, 1970.

————. *Creativity and Perversion.* New York: W.W. Norton, 1984.

————. *The Ego Ideal: A Psychoanalytic Essay on the Malady of the Ideal.* New York: W.W. Norton, 1985.

————. *Sexuality and Mind: The Role of the Father and the Mother in the Psyche.* New York: New York University Press, 1986.

Devereux, Georges. *Essais d'ethnopsychiatrie générale.* Paris: Gallimard, 1970.

Erikson, Erik. "Growth and Crisis of the Healthy Personality." In *Identity and the Life Cycle: Psychological Issues.* New York: International Universities Press, 1959, pp. 50-100.

Fairbairn, W. R. D. *An Object-Relations Theory of the Personality.* New York: Basic Books, 1954.

Friedman, R.C., and Downey, J. "Psychoanalysis, Psychology, and Homosexuality." In *Journal of the American Psychoanalytic Association* 41 (1993): 1159-1198.

Gilligan, Carol. *In a Different Voice: Psychological Theory and Women's Development.* Cambridge, Mass.: Harvard University Press, 1982.

————. "The Conquistador in the Dark Continent: Reflections on the Psychology of Love." *Daedalus* (1984): 75-95.

Green, André. *Narcissisme de vie, narcissisme de mort.* Paris: Minuit, 1983.

————. *Le travail du négatif.* Paris: Minuit, 1993.

Jacobson, Edith. *The Self and the Object World.* New York: International Universities Press, 1964.

Kirkpatrick, Martha, ed. *Women's Sexual Development: Explorations of Inner Space.* New York: Plenum, 1980.

Klein, Melanie. *Envy and Gratitude.* New York: Basic Books, 1957.

————. *The Selected Melanie Klein.* Ed. Juliet Mitchell. New York: Viking Penguin, 1986.

Laplanche, Jean. *Life and Death in Psychoanalysis.* Baltimore: Johns Hopkins University Press, 1976.

Mahler, Margaret. *On Human Symbiosis and the Vicissitudes of Individuation.* Vol. I. *Infantile Psychosis.* New York: International Universities Press, 1968.

McDougall, Joyce. *Plea for a Measure of Abnormality.* New York: International Universities Press, 1980.

————. *Theaters of the Mind; Illusion and Truth on the Psychoanalytic Stage.* New York: Basic Books, 1985.

————. In Elaine Hoffman Baruch and Lucienne J. Serrano. *Women Analyze Women: In France, England and the United States.* New York: New York University Press, 1988, pp.63-84.

Meltzer, Donald. *Sexual States of Mind.* Perthshire: Clunie, 1973.

Money, John. *Lovemaps.* Buffalo, New York: Prometheus Press, 1986.

Person, Ethel. "Some New Observations on the Origins of Femininity." In *Women and Analysis.* Ed. J. Strouse. New York: Viking, 1974, pp. 250-226.

————. "The Erotic Transference in Women and in Men: Differences and Consequences." *Journal of the American Academy of Psychoanalysis* 13 (1985): 159-180.

————. *Dreams of Love and Fateful Encounters: The Power of Romantic Passion.* New York: W. W. Norton, 1988.

Riviere, Joan. "Hate, Greed and Aggression." In *Love, Hate and Reparation*. Ed. M. Klein and J. Riviere. London: Hogarth Press, 1937, pp. 3-53.

Roustang, François. *The Lacanian Delusion*. New York: Oxford University Press, 1990.

Spotniz, Hyman. *Psychotherapy of Preoedipal Conditions: Schizophrenia and Severe Character Disorders*. New York: Jason Aronson, 1976.

Stoller, Robert. *Sex and Gender*. New York: Jason Aronson, 1968.

———. *Perversion: The Erotic Form of Hatred*. Washington, D.C.: American Psychiatric Press, 1968.

———. *Presentations of Gender*. New Haven: Yale University Press, 1985.

Sullivan, Harry Stack. *Personal Pathology: Early Formulations*. New York: W.W. Norton, 1972.

Thompson, Clara. "'Penis Envy' in Women." *Psychiatry* 6 (1943): 123-125.

Winnicott, D. W. "The Depressive Position in Normal Emotional Development." In *British Journal of Psychology* 28 (1955): 89-100.

index

Bleuler, E., 141
Bloom, Harold, 2
Bonaparte, Marie, 15, 76, 138
Borch-Jacobsen, Mikkel, 1, 27
Bordo, Susan, 30
Bowlby, John, 108
Braunschweig, Denise, 25, 157, 158, 159
breasts, 25, 94
    as erogenous zones, 103, 109, 149, 150
bulimia, 19, 104, 105, 106

"The Case of Dora" (Freud), 78
castration, 11, 47, 48, 74-75, 78, 149, 151, 178
castration complex, Freud on, 49, 51-52, 97, 149
Catholicism, 92
Chasseguet-Smirgel, Janine, 17, 24-25, 26, 141-156, 157, 159, 163, 169, 173, 184
Chicago, Judy, 31
childhood, women's connection to, 67
child-rearing, 35
    parental equality in, 23, 26, 93, 109, 131-132, 134,170-171, 174-175
children
    psychoanalysis of, 76, 78-79, 85
    sexuality of, 172
China, 98
Chodorow, Nancy, 23, 33
Christ, 84
Christianity, 84, 92, 145, 151
circumcision, castration and, 151-152
civilization, as masculine, 98
Civilization and its Discontents (Freud), 27
coitus, 14, 61, 62, 63, 94-95
    reproduction and, 110
Confrontation, 126, 127
"The Conquistador of the Dark Continent" (Gilligan), 168
core-gender identity, 173-174
Cornell, Drucilla, 29, 36
countertransference, in psychoanalysis, 79, 162, 176
cultural empathy, 9

cultural literacy, 8

David-Ménard, Monique, 32
de Beauvoir, Simone, 16, 36, 50, 114, 136, 184
deconstructionism, 138
defloration, 97, 149
de Groot, Lampl, 15, 76
Démasquer le réel (Leclaire), 5
depression, 66, 104
Derrida, Jacques, 29, 138
    phallologocentrism on, 9
des femmes [publishing house], 28, 29
desire, 13, 23, 83, 128, 137, 171-172
    narcissism and, 145-146
    of patient, 84-85
Devenir adulte (Lebovici), 102
Devereux, Georges, 7, 180
Diary of a Seducer (Kierkegaard), 15
Didier-Weill, Alain, 1
    interview with, 55-64
    notes on, 13-15
"The Dinner Party" (Chicago), 31
Dinnerstein, Dorothy, 23, 33
Dolto, F., 76
Don Juan, 57, 117, 154
Don Quixote, 154
Dora [Freud's patient], 20, 78

eating disorders, in adolescence, 104
École Normale Supérieure, 126
ego ideal, 144-145
ego psychology, 163
Encore (Lacan), 43
Erikson, Erik, 164
eroticism, 26, 159, 168, 173-174
eternal feminine, 136-137
ethnopsychoanalysis, 6-9, 28, 87-88, 180-181
Eugene Onegin (Pushkin), 29

Fain, Michel, 25, 107, 157, 158, 159
Fairbairn, W.R.D., 164